T0272247

JAMES HILLMAN UNIFORM EDITION

11

Uniform Edition of the Writings of James Hillman
Volume 11: On *Melancholy & Depression*

Series Editor: Klaus Ottmann

Published by Spring Publications

www.springpublications.com


First edition 2024

Cover illustration:
James Lee Byars, *Untitled,* ca.1960. Black ink on Japanese paper.
Estate of James Lee Byars, courtesy Michael Werner Gallery,
New York, London, Berlin

Library of Congress Control Number: 2024947630

ISBN: 978-0-88214-043-8

JAMES HILLMAN

# ON MELANCHOLY

# &

# DEPRESSION

Edited by
TOM CHEETHAM and KLAUS OTTMANN

With an introduction by
KLAUS OTTMANN

SPRING PUBLICATIONS
THOMPSON, CONN.

The Uniform Edition of the Writings of James Hillman
is published in conjunction with

Dallas Institute Publications
The Dallas Institute of Humanities and Culture
Dallas, Texas

as an integral part of its publications program concerned with
the imaginative, mythic, and symbolic sources of culture.

# Contents

# ABBREVIATIONS

*CW = Collected Works of C. G. Jung*, edited and translated by Gerhard Adler and R. F. C. Hull, 20 vols. (Princeton, N.J.: Princeton University Press, 1953–79), cited by paragraph number

*UE = Uniform Edition of the Writings of James Hillman*, 12 vols. (Putnam and Thompson, Conn.: Spring Publications, 2004–)

# INTRODUCTION

Depression is the flaw in love. To be creatures who love, we must be creatures who can despair at what we lose, and depression is the mechanism of that despair. When it comes, it degrades one's self and ultimately eclipses the capacity to give or receive affection. It is the aloneness within us made manifest, and it destroys not only connection to others but also the ability to be peacefully alone with oneself.
—Andrew Solomon, *The Noonday Demon: An Atlas of Depression*

Through depression we enter depths and in depths find soul. Depression is essential to the tragic sense of life. It moistens the dry soul, and dries the wet. It brings refuge, limitation, focus, gravity, weight, and humble powerlessness. It reminds of death. The true revolution begins in the individual who can be true to his or her depression.
—James Hillman, *Re-Visioning Psychology*

This volume of the Uniform Edition of the Writings of James Hillman combines a talk delivered by Hillman in Rome in 1999 on melancholy with an edited transcript of three seminars on the subject of melancholy and depression held at Pacifica Graduate Institute in Carpinteria, California: "In Defense of Melancholy" (1992), "Depressive Syndromes" (1994), and "The Place of Depression in a Manic Civilization" (2000).

Depression is also discussed by Hillman in relation to suicide in his 1964 study *Suicide and Soul*, from an alchemical perspective throughout his writings on *Alchemical Psychology*, and from an archetypal and neoplatonist approach in *Re-Visioning Psychology*. In *Suicide and Soul*, Hillman writes,

> The soul needs the death experience. This can come about through various modes... Suicide is but one of the modes; some

others are depression, collapse, trance, isolation, intoxication and exaltation, failure, psychosis, dissociation, amnesia, denial, pain, and torture. These states can be experienced symbolically or concretely. They can be present in case history or soul history. The mode to psychological experience seems not to matter to the soul providing it has the experience.[1]

For Hillman, these moments of darkness are worth holding on and paying attention to. Borrowing from Freud, who called the interpretation of dreams "the *via regia* to a knowledge of the unconscious element in our psychic life,"[2] Hillman calls depression "the *via regia* of soul-making."[3]

> There is something about feeling the weight of the world. That if you are not depressed with the fish turning belly up in the rivers and the trees being chopped down left and right and the rest of it, you are not living. How could the soul—your soul—not be sensitive to the soul of the world? That is one of the oldest ideas that we have in Western thought, that the soul of the world and the soul of the human being are interconnected. ("Three Seminars")

Hillman approach to depression is twofold:

1. To understand depression less as a disease of the individual than a symptom of our culture: "repression creates depression."

2. To recognize that melancholy is much richer than depression because the latter restricts the soul while the former represents a state of heightened imaginative powers.

Hillman's principle postulate is that we live in a *manic* culture: "We are each subject to the tyranny of a hastened life, a life of merciless acceleration," a culture that has "imprisoned melancholia in the dreaded clinical condition called depression" ("Depression, or Melancholy Without the Gods"). Depression is a symptom of "our culture's addiction to a manic superficiality in growth and movement":[4]

---

1. James Hillman, *Suicide and Soul* (Thompson, Conn.: Spring Publications, 2020 [1964]), 58.

2. Sigmund Freud, *The Interpretation of Dreams,* translated by A.A. Brill (New York: The Modern Library, 1978), 459.

3. "Alchemical Blue and the *Unio Mentalis*," in *UE* 5: 102.

4. James Hillman, *Re-Visioning Psychology* (New York: Harper & Row, 1975), 25.

Depression is still the Great Enemy. More personal energy is expended in manic defenses against, diversions from, and denials of it than goes into other supposed psychopathological threats to society: psychopathic criminality, schizoid breakdown, addictions.[5]

Using archetypal mythology, alchemy, neoplatonist ideas, and the imagery evoked by artists and poets, Hillman shifts his attention away from treating depression as an illness that is within the patient to "the place of depression in a manic society" that "rewards the manic and penalizes the depressed" (Three Seminars"). Alchemically, depression is a *blackening* of the soul. It is the price paid for reflection and insight:

Melancholy has, ever since Aristotle's *Problemata,* been the disease of thinkers. The more white reflection, the more burdened lead; as we produce silver, we increase the lead... We have the feeling of lead poisoning, a state of being swallowed by lead, lost in the lead mine... the depression is the mine... We mine silver from lead, but not to do away with the lead, for that would close down the mine."[6]

Psychotherapy meant to help manage mental conditions and emotional challenges such as depression is itself "a depressive activity":

And if one does not have a connection to the melancholic part of the soul, the melancholic temperament, doing therapy is not going to be easy. ("Three Seminars")

If the gods have become diseases, as Jung has said, "then what you do in psychotherapy is feed the gods. You do not feed them their personal case history... You feed the gods with images." Thus Hillman defines depression as "melancholy without the gods":

Yes, depression may be the endemic disease of our times, but from it the black drops of melancholy may be distilled—drops that are the fundamental medicine for curing the times themselves. For, often, the gods choose melancholy as their means of return.

In a manic society, Hillman argues,

melancholy has not been vanquished or banished. It has gone underground, wears a modern disguise and takes on a modern

5. Ibid., 98.
6. "Silver and the White Earth," in *UE5*: 138.

name: "depression"; and so our medicine and sociology, even national governments and international health organizations have found depression to be the major syndrome of our times and endemic in the Western world's populations. It may be masked, latent, denied, but depression remains a constant, the undertone of our solitude, the void we fear, the bleak loneliness we imagine awaiting at the close of our aging days. ("Depression, or Melancholy Without the Gods")

Hillman cites neoplatonism's approach to "alienation, sadness, and awareness of death, never denying depression or separating melancholy from love and love from intellection":

> It recognized the signal place of imagination in human consciousness, considering this to be the primary activity of the soul. Therefore any psychology that would have soul as its aim must speak imaginatively.[7]

Like neoplatonism, archetypal psychology keeps depression close, "believing that *there* soul is more likely to be served."[8] Depression, therefore, requires a different kind of therapy, "a therapy of ideas" and of images, one that does not drive patients deeper into their miseries but helps them uncover the richness of imagination and leads the soul out of the blackness of depression into the blueness of melancholy towards a *unio mentalis,* a union of spirit and soul:

> We have colored this *unio mentalis* "blue" because the blue we have been encountering transfigures appearances into imaginal realities and imagines thought itself in a new way...When the eye becomes blue, that is, able to see into thoughts and envision them as imaginative forms, then images become the ground of reality.[9]

The goal of Hillman's "therapy of ideas" is to move the soul from its blackening by depression to the kind of poetic beauty that is inherent in melancholy.

> So the job before us is to revert depression back to melancholy. Not to cure depression, not to lick depression and make us happy

---

7. Hillman, *Re-Visioning Psychology,* 198.
8. Ibid., 241.
9. "Alchemical Blue and the *Unio Mentalis,*" 118.

> like the Declaration of Independence says we should be, but
> to increase our understanding of and capacity or melancholy.
> ("Three Seminars")

"We must lift the repression from depression" by taking "an interest in sadness" (Three Seminars). While pharmacological treatments such as antidepressants can provide relief or something close to a cure to the soul of an individual patient, a true and lasting cure can only be achieved by curing the *soul of the world,* in "recognizing the archetypal melancholy in the soul of the world."

> The basic error we all make lies in the subjective focus of the
> depressions we feel—my life, my marriage, my failure, my illness, my aging. The error is personal subjectivity. That we feel
> something does not make it "mine." Depression apart from the
> world's melancholy becomes an utterly selfish preoccupation.
> ("Depression, or Melancholy Without the Gods")

The failure of manic culture thus is to consider depression merely as an *intrasubjective* or *intersubjective* illness:

> Not so long ago the patient's complaint was inside the patient.
> A psychological problem was considered to be intrasubjective... Complexes, functions, structures, memories, emotions—the
> interior person needed realigning, releasing, developing. Then,
> more recently, owing to group and family therapies, the patient's
> complaint was located in the patient's social relations. A psychological problem was considered to be intersubjective; therapy
> consisted in readjusting interpersonal psychodynamics within
> relationships, between partners, among members of families. In
> both modes psychic reality was confined to the subjective. In both
> modes the world remained external, material, and dead, merely a
> backdrop in and around which subjectivity appeared. The world
> was therefore not the province of therapeutic focus.[10]

Hillman instead advocates the restoration of "that particular soul spark" of the *anima mundi* "that offers itself through each thing in its visible

---

10. *"Anima Mundi:* The Return of the Soul to the World," in James Hillman, *The Thought of the Heart and the Soul of the World* (Thompson, Conn.: Spring Publications, 2021 [1992]), 56.

form...its availability to imagination, its presence as a psychic reality."[11] When things are returned to soul, psychic reality no longer depends on experiencing one's self but "upon self-witness of another sort."

> Each particular [psychic] event, including individual humans with their invisible thoughts, feelings, and intentions, reveals a soul in its imaginative display. Our human subjectivity, too, appears in our display. Subjectivity here is freed from literalization in reflexive experience and its fictive subject, the ego. Instead, each object a subject, and its self-reflection is its self-display, its radiance. Interiority, subjectivity, psychic depth—all out there, and so, too, psychopathology.[12]

KLAUS OTTMANN

---

11. Ibid., 61.
12. Ibid., 62.

PART ONE

*Depression, or*
*Melancholy Without the Gods*

Francesco Goya
*Saturn Devouring His Son,* c. 1820–1823
Mural transferred to canvas
Museo del Prado, Madrid

*It is important to realize that this eating the child goes on in your own psyche all the time when something new comes in your mind—a fantasy, an idea, a connection. Whatever the thought, whatever new image, dream, thought comes up in your mind, it is eaten up by the old. This is particularly true for dreams. A dream is a completely fresh spontaneous surprising event, and you eat it up either with a Jungian system or a Freudian system or whatever system you've got, that is Saturn as the old system that eats the new.*

I

To begin reflections on Melancholia, or Dame Melancholy as she was known in earlier times, to think, to speak a word on this theme, we must first reflect upon where we are, the actual daily world that affects our words, the world that speaks through us and compels our words obsessively in a single-minded style from which there may be only one escape—the escape into melancholy itself.

For the style of our lives, and our thoughts, is *manic*. We are each subject to the tyranny of a hastened life, a life of merciless acceleration. The instruments that surround us have become the Penates of our households— the microwave, computer, television remote, kitchen appliances, and the weapons of communication: cellphone, fax and e-mail. Even the medicine cabinet is dedicated to a concerted attack on slowness. The motto on every message is ASAP—as soon as possible. *Fast food, fast track, fast forward;* abbreviated language: *beeps* and *blips,* the *rapido* and *expresso.* Our bathing suit for enjoying a leisurely dip in the sea is now a *Speedo,* and the shoes with which we touch the earth are driving shoes or running shoes. The redemptive vision of secular progress has become a demonic addiction to technical speed.

As Milan Kundera says in his lovely little novel *Slowness,* "Speed is the form of ecstasy the technical revolution has bestowed on man."[1] And, as Aldous Huxley wrote earlier in this century: we moderns have not invented any new sins beyond the seven deadly ones of classical times—except for one: *haste.*

And I, transported here by light, metal wings, and burning jet fuel at super speed to deliver a discourse to strangers (friendly as you may be), a discourse without hesitation, without interruption, to hasten through

A talk delivered at "Arcipelago Malinconia," a convening held at the Teatro Argentina in Rome, November 10–12 1999, and first published as "Malinconia senza Dei" in *Arcipelago Malinconia: Scenari e parole dell'interiorità,* edited by Biancamaria Frabotta (Rome: Donzelli, 2001).

1. Milan Kundera, *Slowness,* translated by Linda Asher (New York: HarperCollins, 1996), 2.

so as to keep within fixed time-limit—and on melancholy! What could more demonstrate our epoch and its manic style! Psychiatry has put the essence of mania into a single defining phrase: "absence of inwardness," which also defines our times.

Thus whatever we say about melancholy is from a position that diametrically opposes it, fears it, hates it, and can only judge it as constrictive depression. Our judgments, even our theories, are fundamentally biased against the very topic of our research by the contemporary mania ruling our collective psyche.

A small but telling example of this manic hatred: In the United States today, morning music broadcast over some radio stations has been computer programmed to select out and censor the minor key, which as the dictionary defines minor, "tends to produce a melancholy effect."

Little wonder that the manifestations of depression present such an insult to the hastened unreflected life. The characteristics of depression force inwardness: slow legs, heavy head and downcast eyes; dull speech; low energy; inattentive concentration and inability to make decisions or take action; guilt and dwelling on the past; shame and a sense of sinfulness; minor persistent physical ailments; constipation and headaches; thoughts of death, abandonment and penury; pessimism and fear of the future; a general distaste of the world, and above all an undertone of sadness; that is, the melancholy mood.

Of course, this stubborn enemy does not go away. Melancholy has not been vanquished or banished. It has gone underground, wears a modern disguise and takes on a modern name: "depression"; and so our medicine and sociology, even national governments and international health organizations have found depression to be *the* major syndrome of our times and endemic in the Western world's populations. It may be masked, latent, denied, but depression remains a constant, the undertone of our solitude, the void we fear, the bleak loneliness we imagine awaiting at the close of our aging days.

Since the manic context of our deliberations fundamentally opposes our theme, we cannot do it justice. As we cannot escape the manic *Zeitgeist*, so we cannot insulate our thought from the pathological diagnostics that have imprisoned melancholia in the dreaded clinical condition called depression.

We will come back to this word "depression," but first we need to linger awhile with acceleration and not pass it by too speedily. The concept "acceleration" belongs not only to physics and technology but has also entered biology. It refers to biological processes, such as early menarche and precocious somatic growth. Young girls today in Western societies in general arrive at puberty two or three, even five or more, years earlier than a hundred years ago, and the growth of human beings has accelerated during the twentieth century so that seats in public transports and sports arenas as well as beds have had to become larger. It is therefore not surprising that accelerated growth in childhood contributes to attention deficit disorders, sexual precocity, and aggressive violence.

Even the celebrity cult belongs to the manic syndrome: quick stardom; fame as notoriety, instead of the slow accumulation of *fama*, or reputation, so treasured in the Renaissance. *Fama*, once a province of ethics and truth, now depends on celerity. But why not? "Celebrity" and "celerity" are cognates.

Though high speed may be high fashion today, it has a classical background, reaching back to Hermogenes of Taurus in the second century of our era whose *Art of Rhetoric*, particularly that section called *Peri Ideōn* (Concerning Ideas), sets forth the language, rhythm and use of celerity. Hermogenes distinguishes between seven kinds of style—gravity, ethos, clarity, beauty, verity, grandeur, and *gorgotes* or *celeritas* (later called *velocitas* and *prestezza*). Renaissance writers such as Antonio Minturno (1564), Johannes Sturm (1570), and Giulio Camillo (fl. 1530) contributed to further differentiation of these styles.

When the seven styles of rhetoric were integrated into the basic cosmic model of the seven planets or seven great gods, speed was assigned to Mars. Celerity suited especially the poetics of battle and of amorous bouts between lovers imagined as sporting warfare. One characteristic of the style was what we would call "clipped" speech; short words and phrases, much as our quick advertising slogans and abbreviations that dominate contemporary communication. In brief, then, as speed rules our manic habits, so Mars, with his haste, rage and eruptive violence and without the ritual constraints that the ancient Romans placed on him, is the god in the major disease of our time. Yes, speed: not depression.

In fact, the reactions to depression in clinical situations show a long history of Martial measures, from the whirling chair and ducking stool into icy water to electroshock. This acute, (read "speedy"—or Martial) approach to the chronic complaint of melancholy includes the well-known impatience, even anger, of the clinician when faced with the unrelenting despair of the depressive patient.

## II

Let us look at a few painted images that I will run through without much psychological or art-historical commentary. My aim is to bring a mood into the room so as to dispel in darkness and silence the manic insanity which so easily overcomes us.

The slides I have collected will show many paintings by mostly famous artists such as Henri Matisse, Paul Cézanne, Vincent van Gogh, Pablo Picasso, Amedeo Modigliani, and also by Spanish, British, and American painters of the later nineteenth and earlier twentieth century. These images present women enclosed in rooms, sitting, reclining, reading, waiting, in reverie by windows or dozing, often their heads to one side, leaning on an arm, a hand, sunk in repose, downcast, immobile.

These paintings show the collective nature of depression—that it is a strand woven into the soul, and exposed especially in the modern Zeitgeist— the lassitude, the immobility, the oppression of women prior to feminist liberation, the object status of the model naked before the creative gaze of the idolized artist, and the oppression of the soul in the family.

A study of nineteenth and early twentieth-century portraits of women would turn up thousands of examples. They confirm our thesis: the generic image states an endemic condition. Depression is in the culture and could not be masked before the eye of the painter.

By attributing the reasons for these paintings to a bourgeois society and a patriarchal culture, we admit that depression is outside the brain and the body, outside the individual psyche, though expressed by individual persons in their bodies.

Were we to look at images of endemic depression, we would more likely find them in the body of the object, like Janet Fish's still life *After Leslie Left*. The scattered remnants of the absent person present the mood,

Janet Fish
*After Leslie Left*, 1983–84
Oil on canvas
The Whitney Museum of American Art, New York
Buffalo AKG Art Museum, Buffalo, N.Y.
© 2024 Janet Fish / Licensed by VAGA at Artists Rights Society (ARS), N.Y.

just as Edward Hopper's bare room, despite bright light, shows despair in the soul of a place. So we could look at the vessels painted by Giorgio Morandi or Nicolas de Stael, the landscapes of Anselm Kiefer, or the late paintings of Mark Rothko in the Houston chapel. The model is gone, the subject is gone, the painter is gone—the invisible world of Hades who had no temple or shrine in the visible world; his kingdom merely suggested, yet deeply overwhelmingly present, the kingdom to which Rothko himself was tempted and finally willingly entered.

In passing, I would like to make one observation about the many figures whose heads are leaning on their hands, their hands drawn to support their heavy heads. This gesture has a long iconic history and belongs not only to women of the nineteenth century. It is a pose of reflection, whether in photographic portraits by Yousuf Karsh or in Rodin's *Thinker.* This pose also provides a profound insight into the nature of melancholy. The hand that reaches into the world, making and doizng, is here drawn as if by a magnet back to the head, withdrawn from the world, making and doing in the mind. The melancholy hand is now sorting and struggling with an interior world of thoughts, worries, anxieties, memories—a hand engaged with mental images.

## III

Because depression is endemic, it resides in the world's *collective* psyche, which transcends your and my personal psyche. A *collective* psyche is more than the additive sum of personal souls. "Collective psyche" is the contemporary term for the world's soul, the *anima mundi.* Therefore, the endemic depression that pervades the world refers to the melancholy that is one of the four great humors, much like one of the four great rivers of Eden at the mythical source of all things, entering in varying degrees into all things. Depression is endemic because melancholy is given with the world as a root component, a cosmic force.

And, as endemic—that is, universal, transpersonal, archetypal—melancholy has its seat not inside our brains, nor can it be reduced to human physiology, even if our human susceptibility to it is subject to clinical and chemical adjustments. Of course, antidepressants, pharmaceuticals, and electroshocks work at ameliorating depressions, but they do not eliminate melancholy that is beyond their reach.

We can witness the endemic melancholy of the world any day or evening: by the seashore, in the dark forest, an empty city street before dawn. The first Gestalt psychologists in the early decades of this century made the radical move of returning emotions to the environment. The world out there has a face, many faces. Gestalt called these faces physiognomic characters. As Wordsworth's famous daffodils dance in the breeze with joy, so other landscapes show sorrow and gloom. These emotions are not projected by the human mind into a "dead" world, but are afforded to the mind by the forms that the soul takes on in the world.

So, when we feel depressed, our moods—unless manically denied—take us to sites of solace and silence, to broken-down, undemanding environ-

*We come eventually to Hopper, one of the great American painters of depression. And the rooms are terribly important, the interior space, that it is held within a space... They are all women, and they are part of the phenomenon of women carrying the depression of the culture, that the people who present depression over the last century and a half were largely women, the cases that turned up in the early years of depth analysis were women, that the suffering soul was carried by women so that they are not only women they are also suffering soul as painted by male painters. From the feminist point of view, it is clear that this is all part of the oppression of women in a patriarchal society. It is also depicting the oppression of the soul and also a depiction of the moods of anima, the moods of the soul... the experience of loss and sadness that men were not supposed to have or were not meant to express. It was all laid onto the other gender as belonging to them.*

ments, old chairs and dim bars, to worn clothes and dumb animals—places and things that partake of melancholy and can harbor it. In much Japanese poetry, the character of a natural place expresses the dejection of mood so that personal feelings of sorrow and gloom need not even be mentioned. Places and things where the world's endemic melancholy wells up and shows its soul help the individual person sustain the weight, partly by communion of mood, partly by recognition that the sorrow is shared by the world, partly by relieving obsessive self-focus.

The world's sorrow? What is this? In mystical traditions this sorrow was carried by the figure of Sophia; in the mystery ceremonies of Eleusis, the sorrow was borne by Demeter; in some Jewish speculations the world is in exile, fallen, the vessels broken, and it will always lie in the vale of melancholy until the Shekhinah descends and the Messiah arrives. Sadness does not result from error, sin or evil; nor is sadness a sign of something "wrong." Rather, sorrow makes compassion possible. It opens the way to accepting the world's inherent suffering and its compassion for us, its creatures. If the world did not want us here, could we last even one day?

The sense that melancholy is in the *world* whereas depression is in *ourselves* makes clearer the enigmatic alchemical statement by Michael Meier, that the journey through the six planetary houses begins in Saturn or lead) and ends in Saturn (or lead).[2] Psychological inwardness begins when we first succumb to depression whether through loss, failure, or heartbreak, or worse through an interior incomprehensible dejection with morbid fantasies. We begin in our personal lead. And the depression reaches its terminal point only with recognition of the archetypal melancholy in the soul of the world.

The basic error we all make lies in the subjective focus of the depressions we feel—*my* life, *my* marriage, *my* failure, *my* illness, *my* aging. The error is personal subjectivity. That we feel something does not make it "mine." Depression apart from the world's melancholy becomes an utterly selfish preoccupation.

To not feel depressed is to not be a member of the planet. To not feel melancholy means utter alienation from the actuality of our times,

---

2. Michael Meier, *Atalanta Fugiens, hoc est, Emblemata Nova de Secretis Naturae Chymica* [The Fleeing Atalanta, i.e., New Chymical Emblems of the Secrets of Nature] (Oppenheim, 1618), Discourse XII.

Auguste Rodin
*The Thinker*, 1881–82 (cast 1884)
Bronze
National Gallery of Victoria, Melbourne
Felton Bequest, 1921

*This position of the head in the hands we will see again and again... You will see this image all the way back to Dürer's* Melencolia, *and you have probably had this yourself for hours and hours—your head too heavy to hold up.*

and therefore, as I have insisted for many years, depression is a political statement, a protest in the soul against environmental misery, an adequate response to the pathological destruction going on in the daily world.

As innumerable species of plants and animals go extinct each day, and leave this planetary garden forever, and after eons of evolution brought them to their perfection, this massive biocide suggests that endemic depression may be co-reactive to the loss of species and impoverishment of the earth. As long as you and I share the same terrain, the same air and bio-mass with these fading and disappearing creatures, as well as the disappearing languages, customs, skills, stories, memories, and arts of indigenous peoples, of course, at some level of the soul, you and I are in mourning. As the world soul grieves its losses, so the collective levels of our souls mourn.

Beyond these visible losses, there is a loss more profound, the loss implied by such words as "secular," "rational," "human," "modern," "scientific"—the loss of the gods, not only Dame Melancholy and Saturn but, in particular, Hades, the god of loss, the god who lives in the void. Hades who annuls all constructions, resides in the invisible, the god not mentioned but invisibly present in Freud's theory of depression as a phenomenon of loss and mourning.

As the world exterior to us is reflected in our depressions, so therapy of these states may also call upon the world. Two examples may suffice:

Earlier, in the mid-Renaissance, for instance, depression could be treated in a light, gentle, and sweet manner—a treatment under the guidance of Venus. A light diet of fresh eggs, salads, young meats, grapes—foods with moisture. Green, white, and yellow liquids were to be added to the body's baths. And since melancholy clings to thick, dark, bad-smelling air, a person could ward off the enveloping cloud of mood by having flowers in the rooms and wearing a sweet smelling potion, sometimes shaped like an apple, in a pendant around the neck.

Another mode called for travel. English melancholics in the eighteenth century were often sent abroad, especially to Italy, in the company of a therapist-tutor-scholar to visit places of antiquity, frequent galleries of classic painting, and walk among the ruins. Personal depression was expanded backward to past grandeur and outward to the melancholy landscapes of overgrown deserted temples and broken columns. This was a therapy more under the tutelage of Jupiter. Even as late as 1870, the French psychiatrist Louis-Florentin Calmeil advised visits to museums.

The value of these earlier ideas of treatment may lie less in their literal application than in their ability to nourish the starved imagination. Saturn's images of skulls, tombs, dungeons, and catacombs; Venusian images of colored fluids and flowers; images from classic texts of myth and tragedy, courageous epics; ruined monuments.

Without the images, we have only depression describing itself in the language of clinical psychology with taxonomies of "reactive," "neurotic," "endogenous," "paranoid," "delusional," "bi-polar,"etc., degrees and kinds of depression. "Depression is the absence of the mirth reflex," says one definition; "general retardation of all bodily and psychic functions," says another; "mourning for a lost object," says a third.

Ideas of melancholy in medieval times instead offered images. Acedia, for example. This affliction descended particularly on monks who lay abed and could not bake bread or toil in the vineyards, would not rise for prayers, and were prey to the aridity of spirit. Acedia was imaged by a dog, a pig, and a goat. The thin, curled dog in Dürer's *Melencolia I* refers back to that dog of acedia.

So any of us curled on our beds in despairing introspection, chasing our own tails, or tails cringing with shame, sucked dry by the fleas and lice of persistently biting scruples could feel the presence of the image and could sympathize with the mood by means of an image apart from the effects of the mood. Images give focus, distance—even a glimmer of impersonal objectivity. Anyone who has lived in a household with a depressed member can feel the presence of the pig that demands so much space, takes so much into her or his self, that oppressive weight that seems to fill all the rooms, as well as the disorder, even decline into filth.

Other images, associated especially with Saturn, often called the "God of Melancholy," were animals of thick skin, dull color, slow movement, or that lived long years, such as the elephant, tortoise, solitary moose of dark swamps and woods, and the camel dutifully bearing her burdens through the parched featureless desert. Also owls of the night and blackbirds whose voices forecast disaster. These images can be addressed by means of imagination and can give voice to meanings.

Albrecht Dürer
*Melencolia I,* 1514
Engraving
The Metropolitan Museum of Art, New York
Harris Brisbane Dick Fund, 1943

*Look at the hand where that hand is holding the head up... That is the
classical image of melancholy from Dürer. Now remember the stare
we saw in Goya's popping eyes—this is this tremendous obsessed stare.
You can see how intensely the mind is working. This is not passive
aggressive. This is a* furor melancholicos. *It is very important to
realize how active the classical idea of melancholy was that the mind
was intensely active like rage.*

# IV

We come now to the very root of the depression endemic to our times; I will even risk saying its very cause.

If behind our personal depressions is the archetypal figure, humor, or cosmic force—Melancholy—then let us point directly, as we come to the close of this millennium, and also of these reflections this morning, to the reason Melancholy takes its specific depressive form in our modern times. The clue is given by the title of this symposium: "Archipelago Melancholia."

What are these scattered islands? What holds them together in the image of an archipelago?

Does the image refer to different isolated viewpoints, languages, cultures, professions—clinical, physiological, societal, literary? Or does this imaginative phrase reveal the nature of depression as a *phenomenon of islands*, the common human spirit captivated by insularity?

It is, I have come to believe, the concentration upon the islands rather than participation in the common sea that originates much of our modern misery, an isolation that the very word "island" connotes. No networking by Web and Internet, no intensified human relationships or support groups, not even the bridges built by personal love and family bondings can remedy the basic logic and ontology of the self-enclosed monadic structure of islands.

We are now close to our ending, yet we need to introduce a logical distinction from philosophy—though it is a flaw in dramatic form to bring on stage a new character in the third act, and we are in the third act. Nonetheless, it is relevant to distinguish logically between external and *internal* kinds of relations. Depression or melancholy? Which is it? This depends on how we conceive the logic of the archipelago.

The relations between particulars, such as islands, may be understood as external to them. A third factor—a web, a thread, a bridge—may link one to another. Such relations, because they, too, are external, then require not only to be constructed and maintained as psychotherapy proposes and teaches; but further, they logically require a binding independent factor that provides the relation between the bridge and the islands linked by the bridge, *ad infinitum*. Thus Heidegger can say a bridge not only binds the two sides of a river, but, because it is external to the river, the bridge also separates them, creates the isolation of the two banks.[3] The logic of external relations leaves each island ontologically separate, distinct and alone—and depressed.

Internal relations, philosophers say, are those in which the islands inherently belong one to the other. The islands imply each other, they are co-dependent, co-relative, so that you cannot conceive of one without the other.

For instance, in human affairs a marriage is more than an external relationship between two individuals. At the moment of marriage, the two become internally related: the idea "wife" implies "husband" and vice versa. They are joined by immersion in what surrounds them: the archetypal sacrament of marriage and not merely the bridge of their relationship. Marriage converts the external relationship of a pair of individuals before the wedding into a union of co-dependents. The wedding formalizes the internal relation of the couple, revealing their internal affinity and announcing the impossibility of internal separation.

Thus we can relate only when the relationship is internal, already given, a pre-existent third, an internality they share. For this logical reason relationships cannot be made no matter how hard we try. They can only be discovered.

# V

"Ascoltate ancora," says Eugenio Montale in his "Lettera levantina," "voglio svelarvi qual filo/unisce le nostre distanti esistenze."[4] Is not the thread internal to the spider. Is it not there prior to her leap into space, the internal connection brought forth, externalized by distance.

So, in regard to our archipelago, what is already pre-existent to the distance between the islands is the common sea that holds all islands in its embrace, that same sea that laps the shores and erodes the beaches. Our isolated individualities are internally related through that sea. When

---

3. "Building Dwelling Thinking," in Martin Heidegger, *Poetry, Language, Thought,* translated by Albert Hofstadter (New York: Harper Colophon Books, 1975), 152ff.

4. "Listen again. I want to uncover the thread/that unites our distant beings," in *Otherwise: Last and First Poems of Eugenio Montale,* translated by Jonathan Galassi (New York: Random House, 1984), 104–5.

we imagine ourselves immersed in that sea, rather than risen out of it, then the archipelago becomes a geographical sisterhood rather than a mere scatter of rocky promontories, each with its own lighthouse, and then melancholia becomes the flowing base of black water, a continuing foundation that all islands share, as our very animal bodies are preponderantly composed of that sea.

This sea was originally named *oceanus*, of endless horizons, sucking depths and indomitable currents; Oceanus, θεῶν γένεσιν,[5] in Homer's words, genesis of the gods themselves, ground of all being, girdling the earth and encircling all existence like a great serpent as Oceanus was often depicted. And this serpent, this oceanic foundation, one of whose streams is the thick, dark, slow, cold and very deep current, melancholy, given with the psyche itself, for Oceanus was, as the extraordinary philologist R. B. Onians says, "the primal cosmic ψχή [psyche]."[6]

The soul on its island of subjectivity knows melancholy only as lonely despair and bleak outlook. It has removed itself from the supportive embrace of the sea, so that the sea reflects only the soul's isolation in introspective subjectivity, that is, depression.

Coleridge in his great ode, "Dejection," casts his eye over the entire horizon spread before him, but locked in his isolation he writes "I see, not feel."[7] His is the voice of Romantic longing to restore the unifying thread of existence, severed by modern self-centered isolation.

The way of return from personal depression to universal melancholy is by coming down from the heights, descending to the shoreline—the direction that depression anyway urges—and listening to voices other than our own obsessionally personal cogitations: my misery, my dejection, me.

T. S. Eliot writes at the end of his "Prufrock" poem:

> I shall... walk upon the beach.
> I have heard the mermaids singing, each to each.
> I do not think they will sing to me.

---

5. *Iliad* 14.201 and 304: "from whom the gods are sprung" (trans. A. T. Murray).

6. Richard Broxton Onians, *The Origins of European Thought: About the Body, the Mind, the Soul, the World, Time, and Fate* (Cambridge: Cambridge University Press, 1951), 249.

7. "Dejection: An Ode," in Samuel Taylor Coleridge, *Selected Poems* (New York and Avenel, N.J.: Gramercy Books, 1996), 72.

> I have seen them riding seaward on the waves
> Combing the white hair of the waves blown back
> When the wind blows the water white and black.[8]

No, they do not sing to the "me" because the "me" is the consciousness of an island. Yet, and still, and perhaps forever, the mermaid daughters of Oceanus beckon.

Virginia Woolf, depressed, or haunted by melancholy—which one?—walked into that sea, perhaps to find the source of that melancholy, to enter its deep home.

With your indulgence I would like to quote from one more poet, Matthew Arnold. His "Dover Beach" is one of the most powerful and well-known poems in the English language, and with it I shall bring my reflections to an end.

He, too, stands at the shore:

> Listen! you hear the grating roar
> Of pebbles which the waves suck back, and fling,
> At their return, up the high strand,
> Begin, and cease, and then again begin,
> With tremulous cadence slow, and bring
> The eternal note of sadness in.
>
> Sophocles long ago
> Heard it on the Ægean, and it brought
> Into his mind the turbid ebb and flow
> Of human misery...

Then Arnold explains why the human misery: Not because of the "eternal note of sadness" that belongs with the sea. Not the sea itself. Not Oceanus, the primal psyche, the endemic collective, generator of the gods. But the loss of the gods, which leaves the islands high and dry, and ourselves subject to a melancholy without the gods:

> The sea of faith
> Was once, too, at the full, and round earth's shore
> Lay like the folds of a bright girdle furled.

---

8. "The Love Song of J. Alfred Prufrock," in *The Poems of T. S. Eliot*, vol. 1: *Collected and Uncollected Poems*, edited by Christopher Ricks and Jim McCue (Baltimore: Johns Hopkins University, 2015), 9.

> But now I only hear
> Its melancholy, long, withdrawing roar,
> Retreating, to the breath
> Of the night-wind, down the vast edges drear
> And naked shingles of the world.

"Dover Beach" could have concluded with those "drear and naked shingles," that "melancholy, long, withdrawing roar" as the gods retreat. But Arnold's last stanza opens into prophecy. Though written in 1866, he predicts the three devastating consequences in the human world so apparent today when the gods are not recognized and Dame Melancholy not honored:

> Ah, love, let us be true
> To one another! For the world, which seems
> To lie before us like a land of dreams,
> So various, so beautiful, so new,
> Hath really neither joy, nor love, nor light,
> Nor certitude, nor peace, nor help for pain;
> And we are here as on a darkling plain
> Swept with confused alarms of struggle and flight,
> Where ignorant armies clash by night.[9]

Melancholy without the gods leaves us, *first*, in environmental disaster on the "darkling plain" of a desolate world, its beauty only a delusion. Thus, *second*, we turn to idealized human relationships—"Ah, love let us be true / To one another!" expecting human love to replace the world's love—and thus we are always disappointed and always in search. The final prophecy of "Dover Beach" states, *third*, that without the tempering inwardness of melancholy the senseless violence, the "ignorant armies" of Mars are unleashed.

Yes, depression may be the endemic disease of our times, but from it the black drops of melancholy may be distilled—drops that are the fundamental medicine for curing the times themselves. For, often, the gods choose melancholy as their means of return.

---

9. Matthew Arnold, "Dover Beach, "*https://www.poetryfoundation.org/poems/43588/dover-beach.*

PART TWO

*Three Seminars
on Melancholy & Depression*

## Clinical Education

I want to make it clear from the beginning that we are not in a training course. You can get clinical training everywhere. It is offered by all sorts of institutions, and there are training programs for all the various schools of psychotherapy. I am interested here in clinical education. Clinical education is something different from other kinds of education, just as education is something different from training. Since this is called clinical education it means we are not going to be training you in "what to do with...," and "how do you meet...," and "what are your techniques for...," and "what are the procedures...," and "what is the process...," and the rest of it. A lot of that belongs to training. We will talk about the psychiatry of depression, but we are not involved in a training program. We are involved in an education day, or two or three.

One of the aims of education as I understand it is the expansion of your subjectivity so that there is more space for receiving. An educated person has a wider framework. So, one of the things we will be doing is working on the education of your subjectivity in regard to what is called depression. So that you can take it in. Because if you not have that expansion you cannot take in what is presented to you and you are going to work against what you are confronted with—both your own depression and another person's depression. Taking in the other person is difficult, and taking in depression is even more difficult. And no amount of training alone will do. Training can give you the *techné*, the *praxis* for that, but it is really a matter of education. How do you understand—the way we use the word understand—how do you take in, how do you receive this, what is your framework for reception?

The following is based on a transcript of three seminars held at Pacifica Graduate Institute in Carpinteria, California: "In Defense of Melancholy" (1992), "Depressive Syndromes" (1994), and "The Place of Depression in a Manic Civilization" (2000); edited for clarity and length, with footnotes added for references made by Hillman during his seminars.

Another part of clinical education as I see it is the refinement of sensitivity. Now training does bring that out because you are supposed to be more perceptive in what you are seeing and you learn more careful and more clever responses, but that is only part of it. There is something else, having to do with the refinement of the imagination of feeling. The *imagination* of feeling, not just feeling. The imagination of feeling has to do with imagining the feeling in the other person or in the condition. One of the great complaints in personal relationships is that you are not imagining where I am. We say "You are not feeling where I am," but the point is that you cannot imagine it! So part of clinical education is the development of, or the working on, the imagination of feeling. There is a distinction here somewhere and I do not know quite what it is, but it seems to me you cannot truly empathize or *feel into* without some imagination of what it feels like, or what the imagination of the other person is. Or even falling in love with your imagination of the other person's imagination. Being really caught by that imagination, then your feeling will flow with that. So I am putting the imagination before feeling in this context of education.

What else goes with clinical education as distinct from training? And I am not putting down training, but we should see that training is a piece of larger thing called clinical education. It is one of the ways you do develop perceptions, you do develop expanded subjectivity. You are taught to pay attention to where you are yourself with your subjectivity with regard to the other person, which is called countertransference now. Another part of clinical education I would think is interiority. These are all really closely connected. It is a question of getting into the case. Getting into it with your perceptions, your insights, getting into the interiority of what iss going on, getting into the interiority as a penetration, as a partly imaginative but also a prolonged interest into what is there so that you are getting into it more and more. You can call it deepening. This leads to something which is again different from training. It is a knowledge in the biblical sense of "intercourse with." Being really close to what you are dealing with. That is not the same as allopathic medicine where you are opposed to what you are dealing with, that is, where you find countermeasures. This is getting so close to it that you become like it or you enter into it, you become intimate with it. That kind of knowledge is clinical education.

The old asylum psychiatrists, the people who invented the field of psychiatry in the nineteenth century, and even earlier, at the end of the eighteenth century, lived in the asylums with their patients. They did not have a consulting room where their patients crossed town in a subway to come see them for an hour. They lived in the confines, sang in the religious choruses on Sunday, went to the same church services, and raised their children in the asylum. The psychiatrists of the period are the ones that gave us all these terms and the definitions and the diagnostics that have been boiled down and bastardized in the DSM.[1] But the basic language of psychiatry comes from an intimacy with the patient; from being immensely close to, interested in, and alive to the presentation of the images that the patient is producing. So it is a constant intercourse or intimacy with—a knowledge of. Learning to have that kind of knowledge is what I think clinical education is about. We are putting together two kinds of words that are not usually put together. You usually have "clinical training" and "academic education." I am saying all this in the beginning to lay out what I want to be doing, and also to tell you the attitude I have towards what we are doing so that you are not disappointed by imagining you are going to get something else.

Also, culture goes with clinical education. Jung gave the simplest definition of neurosis. He said that neurosis is one-sided consciousness. He also said that it is inauthentic suffering. It is not real suffering but substitute suffering. One-sided consciousness is really a consciousness that is locked into a rigidity of culture. It does not have enough culture, enough extension, enough depth, height. It is a cultural narrowness. Culture is something that is multi-layered like a compost heap. It is fermenting. It is complicated, not simple. It is sophisticated. It is twisted. That is a part of clinical education: twisting the knowledge, the information, you already have, so it becomes more cultured. It is about culturing your information. We have lost the distinction between information and knowledge. We think that the accumulation of information is equal to knowledge. I think they have very little to do with each other. We have more and more information and people know less and less. The quicker the learning process, it seems the lower the SAT scores. Something strange is happening in the

---

1. The *Diagnostic and Statistical Manual of Mental Disorders*, now in its fifth edition (DSM-5-TR), is published by the American Psychiatric Association.

confusion of information and knowledge. Knowledge is complexity. It is an interwoven complexity that produces a depth of feeling and thought. It allows thinking more deeply, feeling more deeply, a depth of history, beauty, imagery (connecting beauty and imagery together), so that these things I have discussed now under clinical education all fit together in different ways.

Freud made out something important in the very beginning when he wrote his little book on lay analysis[2] (which he was in favor of), saying psychoanalysis is not a medical profession, meaning that it is not a literal profession of healing or curing. He wrote that anyone can become clinically educated. It benefits enormously to be in clinical situations and to see the actual carriers of these conditions. You do not see them very much now because they are drugged so quickly that everybody's the same, and you do not see the beautiful differentiation that made up nineteenth-century psychiatry where you could subtly tease apart all the disorders of the mind, the peculiarities of the psyche. But still, the point is that the clinical belongs in a larger cultural picture, and it is a language that many people can learn.

I think there is a direction all the way through psychology in the people thinking—*thinking*—about psychotherapy: Wilfred Bion, Erik Erikson, and Erich Fromm, relating it to society. Freud did that too, early on. It is basic in Alfred Adler, and it is been there in the leading thinkers. But the DSM does not represent the leading thinkers, although there are a lot of them who wrote the book—how many I do not know. It is very important, that sense of the societal aspect, but also the philosophical aspect and the archetypal background to what one is seeing and saying.

I hope that you are able to see that you can place the clinical, with all its language and all its empirical examination and all its diagnostic differentiation, into a larger context. You can bring in all those categories and all that psychiatric history and place it within a cultural context so that you do not take it all literally. You take it all in, you learn it all, but it is not the truth. The truth is placed within a context. That is the difference between being a trained clinician and being an educated clinician. And anyone can be an educated clinician. You can understand these categories

---

2. Sigmund Freud, *The Question of Lay Analysis: An Introduction to Psycho-Analysis*, translated by Nancy Procter-Gregg (London: Imago Publishing, 1947).

and use them as ways of viewing people and the world and not only as tools, diagnostic tools, or literal techniques for labeling. One of the difficulties with training in most institutions is that it is culture-free. In other words, the culture is just accepted: "This is the way it is." We are in the free-market, multicultural, capitalist democracy—all the various soubriquets that are supposed to be the way we are. But training does not place the view of the patient or the view of the illness within a cultural milieu.

### The Manic Context

So you see that the first thing we have to say about depression, or about melancholy, is that we are looking at it in our culture, from our culture's point of view. And ours is a manic culture. The fact that I am even here, that I flew at five or six hundred miles an hour to a place I do not know, then get off a plane and start talking to people I do not know is manic. It is a little bit insane, a bit manic. You do not have to know to whom you are talking if you are manic, you just have to talk. The main thing for the manic speaker is that nobody should interrupt because that makes you very angry. There should be no interruptions and no disturbances and there is no particular logic to the talk. It is a flight of ideas, as they call it, one thing just follows another through free associations, whatever comes into your mind, whatever sound you hear. A little bit like John Cage's music. If some little noise comes in from outside, then that gets incorporated into it too as long as it keeps moving.

What I want to do is frame depression within this civilization's manic condition. We need to think about the depression of the culture and what to do about it and where it is and where it is in you when you are subject to those terrible dark slowing times.

What we are now engaged in is a manic event and it does not even feel as if this is unusual. But our way of life is manic, from one end to the other: from the fast cut of our films, from the rock music, from the rap music, from surfing the channels, the PiP (Picture in Picture) on TV—do you have one of those? One picture in another picture, so you can watch two shows at the same time—the aerobics, the fast food, not having enough sleep. The United States is now concerned with too much food and too little sleep. People are not in danger of drunken drivers on the highways but of people who fall asleep on the highways right in the middle of the manic life. On the highway, depression strikes by putting you to sleep, stopping everything. The loss of the night. In the centers of our contemporary manic culture like Las Vegas, there is no night. And the fact that in the last ten years the number of people who fly on airplanes has gone up by, what, forty percent? I have not even mentioned the computer, the web, the net, fax, email, the PalmPilot, the laptop. I have not mentioned the sudden irritability. The numbers of people who carry a revolver in the glove compartment—this is now Texas mainly—and it is ready at any moment, sudden irritable shooting. People shoot each other in gyms—basketball players, squash-court people. Did you know for example, that morning music on some radio stations in the US, the way they play the music—they have removed any music written in a minor key. You do not start the day in a minor key. Quite extraordinary. Only major keys in the morning. And how much coffee and sugar and speed? And also the TV commercials. Have you ever watched a kid's program on Saturday morning? Not only the commercials, but the speed with which everything happens—the cartoons. You notice it particularly when you come from Europe and watch American TV. Of course, it is partly because we have to condense more of the advertisement into a shorter amount of space. It is economically governed, they say, but the speed of it is incredible.

Now this manic way of living is appropriate probably to a society that is top-dog. How do you stay on top? How do we think that you stay on top? By staying in the fast lane. By keeping active, keeping young, keeping fast. Underdog societies are usually depressive, subdued, submissive, suppressed—so it may be there. Perhaps there is complete harmony between the fact of the manic civilization and the being on top. Which is why we fear economic depression to such an extraordinary extent that we do not even use the word any more. It belongs to the 1930s. We now talk about recession, perhaps stagflation, perhaps severe recession, but the word depression does not come up economically. So when we ask where is the depression in the society besides where is it in you, could we not find it in many other places such as in the aged, in the ghettos, in bankruptcies (enormous numbers of bankruptcies), in alcohol, in women? In the religious sense of sin, in the fact that so many people join so many religions in order to overcome the sense of sin—to find redemptive ways out of the sense of sin? And in body aches? The aching body—you know the ad slogan "I do not have time for the pain." So we have now on the nonprescription shelves in the drug store every possible pain killer you can imagine that ten or fifteen years ago were prescription drugs.

This is almost built into American culture. It is something strange though, the signs you see on the highway: All You Can Eat. Save by Buying Now. We celebrate the holidays with giant consumer sales. The throwaway of our materials—throwaway pens, throwaway razor blades. Throwaway—this is a manic way of living. In the movies, the manic hero never sits down to eat. You never see manic people eating. Or sleeping. Mel Gibson is never laying down in a movie unless he is shot. And the vitamins that we take are to increase performance. And the words we use are more and more manic: megabytes, megadoses, megabucks. The soundbite is manic. The amount of electrical power that is used in the country that requires the nuclear industry is partly to keep the dark away. How many office buildings are lit all night long? It always amazes me—I cannot believe there are that many cleaning crews in these forty-story buildings. Floor after floor there are lights on. Always Open, Never Closed—another one of the signs. These are all manic slogans. In the early morning, what are we doing? We are not shuffling around, looking for this and that, and you know how it is in the early morning, how you actually feel—but we are doing aerobics to some idiot on the TV. Now these are all manic habits. What most of us say is that we do not have enough time. On the TV, we watch racing and crashing cars, guns, flames, reckless driving, rapid fire sales talk. And I have left out a lot of other things like video games and casino gambling, and rush and hurry and time flying and so on. So, of course, a lot of things become the enemy. Menopause becomes the enemy—the very word "pause" that is in there.

Also our athletics. Every four years we have all new records. People are moving faster than they were four years ago. Jumping farther, leaping higher, and running more quickly. Breaking the record does not have anything to do with style or grace, it has to do with speed. I do not need to mention the TV, the surfing, watching several channels at once. I do not even have to switch anymore. I can just see it all happening together. And that promotes the flight of ideas that is one of the three major symptoms of hypermania or full-blown mania. Flight of ideas. The acceleration of all psychic processes. "Acceleration" is the word also used in demography and biological notions of human growth. In the last one hundred years we have had something called acceleration. That is, that puberty arrives earlier, and people grow more quickly, taller, and faster. Acceleration has affected the whole physical reality of our bodies. If in the late nineteenth century, puberty or menses came between fifteen and seventeen years of age, it now arrives between eleven and thirteen—that is a huge shift. It is called acceleration.

Now all these things are easy enough to see and familiar enough. I mention them so that you realize the prejudice with which each of us goes at the moments of depression in our own lives. That it is a severe interruption of the manic life, and therefore our judgments about depression—and I am using that word now in the clinical sense, the narrow sense—our judgments about it are going to be negative, are going to be assaultive. As you know that when you yourself are depressed, you punish yourself. There is a punisher, a cruel punisher who attacks your depression. If you do not get it from the outside, you get it from within your own psyche. We carry our punisher within us.

Even people getting older—well, we are having an active old age! The kind of life you are supposed to live when you are getting older is to deny the fact that you are depressed, melancholic, slow, heavy, and sad, but that you maintain a kind of perpetual *mobilaise* for as long as you can go. Keep going. Geriatric sex is a whole new field in psychotherapy now.

PRS! It will be in the next edition of the DSM! Post-Retirement Slow-down. Very difficult to face. It seems to be a wasteland. The man faces the difficulties of life after retirement or at the moments of retirement, because it feels slowed down and empty and the temptation is to look for every opportunity to fill his life again. To be busy, active.

It is important that even as we may joke, as we notice the manic condition, it just builds up underneath. This is really a tragic way to live—especially for children—especially to foist this onto children. This, among all the other things we foist onto them, like hunger—we foist this onto them too—those Nintendo games, the speed!

There are a lot of other little things that indicate the manic quality. The difficulty we have with mourning, the fact that recovery groups are trying to bring grief back into the society as if it were not always there. The sense of too much input. Do you have that a sense of too much coming in? The fax, the modem, call waiting, the cell phone in the car, multichannels on TV—this tremendous input of the hyperactivity of information and access. Now with all that, if you get depressed, you are out of the loop. You are out of the network. You are dead.

Ignorance of history is part of the manic syndrome. It is also part of psychopathy. One of the crucial facts about the psychopath is that he learns nothing from experience, that has no remorse. When Mr. Bush could not apologize to the Japanese for Hiroshima after the Japanese apologized for the attack in Pearl Harbor—that is an inability to carry remorse. We do no wrong, we just go on to the next thing. Diagnostically, I do not know whether we call this psychopathy or mania. But the point is very important: that perhaps memory is one of the most important civic activities that we need to reintroduce, which we have been doing slowly regarding Vietnam. And the Vietnam Memorial,which is a very, very heart-rending place, is one of the first steps in something like that. Designed by a young woman, by a woman of another ethnic background—how that got through Congress no one knows![3] And its importance in the heart of the nation is key, especially in view of all those white, erect buildings in Washington. But the problem with memory is that we remember in strange victorious ways. The dark side of memory is kept back. What a struggle it has been to bring out the veterans that were injured by our own weapons. What a struggle it has been to recognize how our smart bombs were dumb. How difficult it is to remember. You see, memory requires a kind of attitude of wanting...what? The whole truth? Wanting all of it? I do not know quite what. Memory as memory of victory is not memory. It is part of memory. And remember memory, *Mnemosyne*, is the mother of the Muses. And there are many modes of remembering. The arts are modes of remembering. So, of course, part of the same paranoid plot that is going on in the country is to stop funding the arts.

I do believe that we are anesthetized. Robert Lifton's idea of psychic numbing is true, and I think it is very difficult not to be numbed because of the tremendous input that assaults us.[4] Not only because of our history,

---

3. The Vietnam Veterans Memorial in Washington D.C. was designed by American architect Maya Lin and opened in 1982.

4. Robert Jay Lifton, "Beyond Psychic Numbing: A Call to Awareness," *American Journal of Orthopsychiatry* 52, no. 4 (October 1982): 619–29.

but if you are on the TV all day long, you would be exhausted. You have to shut out an enormous amount of the day because of the sensations and perceptions that assault you.

Now if you came from another culture, say a culture that has been depressed for four hundred years, like it has in Turkey or Portugal, from a place that once had a great empire and then collapsed, and you watched our TV, what would you think is happening? Cars crashing, gigantic flames, guns, rushing around, reckless driving, sales talk at a tremendous speed, especially people who sell mattresses and cars and furniture—rapid fire. The manic has a martial quality. I am using the word for the god Mars who is the god of fire and speed among other things. Part of an old style in ancient psychiatry of treating the Saturnian—and Saturn is the god of melancholy—is to use Mars against Saturn. That is, to use violence and power and speed to rev up the lead. So we are watching this, and our kids are watching this, and we have an entire generation of hyperactive people, not just the kids on whom it is blamed, but all of us in the way we live it. The way I am talking is manic. I am talking much too fast for us to absorb what is being said. But there is a compulsion or an impulse to talk quickly because you might get bored. You see the defense right in the room. And getting bored is the worst thing that could happen. There should not be pauses. There should not be anything wasted. Everything needs to keep moving. We have got to get this country moving again!

Now, one of the really major semiconscious statements that people make: "I do not have time." "I did not get to it." "I cannot do it." "There is not enough time." I have to do this, and there is not enough time. I cannot get it all done in a day. I cannot do all that I have to do. So one is in a hurry or rushing, or trying to find two hours of what is called quality time. And then there is the guilt that comes when I flake out in front of the TV set unable to make another move. That sense that when it stops, it is dead, wasted, boring, useless—now that is manic too. The manic condition does not brook anything that stops it. It does not want stopping, and it does not want interference or interruption. So the only thing that works to stop it is to catch a cold or to get a symptom or to have some sort of "problem," as people say, which sets up an obstacle to the onward rush of the day and of the night.

The simplest key for recognizing a manic condition is the old description from classical psychiatry: you have an elation of feeling, a hyperactivity of willing, and flights of thinking. Not consistent logical step-by-step thinking, but thinking that is a flash. Just imagine: that is what an entire civilization is attempting to have in us—an elation of feeling, to be up. Hyperactivity of willing: to be able to get it all done in a day. And flights of thinking, or what in the Renaissance was called the rhetoric of speed, which belonged to Mars. Certain rhythms in poetry and certain kinds of words, and short sentences, produce manic bursts of mind.

And because of this speed there is also an absence of history. Somebody said you are in the same generation as anybody who is either seven years younger or seven years older than you, so we have roughly fourteen-year generations. But now the generation of Windows 2000 is only five years—1995 and now 2000. And the appearance of new generations of all kinds of technology and equipment has sped up tremendously. Even making new animals like cloned sheep or pigs is again a speed phenomenon. Something fundamental in the way we think of history is happening there. And the new comedians who stand up without any history, who have no Catskill Jewish background, who simply tell about what happened that afternoon in the supermarket with the check-out girl. Or their mother-in-law or some bits of trivia—the absence of history and the speed of the no-stopping speech is part of this kind of way to be funny.

Now in personality types, manic people, hyper-manic people are supposed to be outgoing, vivacious, optimistic, and suggestible, often argumentative so you do not want to interfere, but mainly out-going, optimistic, in a high mood. "How are you?" "Fine! Couldn't be better!" This kind of euphoric aggression is something that we are supposed to admire. You know, "How are *you*?!" The man who lived next to me in Dallas was an African American, as the whole little neighborhood was. I would say, "How are you today?," and he would say something like, "I am still trying." And that was enough, you know. And the movement on the street was quite extraordinary because at noon, in Dallas, it gets pretty hot even in March, straight through to November. And the young downtown businessmen would be out there jogging, and the Black neighbors would be walking in that heat in a way where there was no movement. There was no sweat. It was absolutely beautiful movement, and here are these insane, manic people running through the same streets. But they were ahead! They had the money! They were victorious. They were on top. That is what I mean about the culture that rewards the manic and penalizes the depressed.

Also in classical psychiatry the manic condition, generally speaking, involves a speeding up of all psychic processes. Now, can you transfer that description to the civilization as a whole? Now if you can, where and how are you going to receive depression? How can you even think about it? How can you enter it? How can you give it space, or place, or value, or heart? How can you give heart to the melancholy temperament in this kind of a civilization? And what happens to the people who do live the melancholy style? The homeless, the Native Americans on their reservations, the people in the inner cities, the old. What happens to those who are not quite making it in the manic style? Already there is a political implication here.

I think that is what Huxley[5] meant by saying that the only sin we have added is haste. Transportation, for example, went at the same rate of speed from Alexander to Napoleon. Armies moved no quicker in Napoleon's time than they did in Alexander's. But with the beginning of the railroad, things began to move more quickly. The improvement of roads made a difference, but not that big a difference between Napoleon's time and Roman times. The idea that things are speeding up is an archetypal idea that is expressed in Indian thought as the Kali Yuga. We are now in the Kali Yuga. As the world moves towards its end in the cycle everything speeds up—it is an ancient fantasy. Whether its true or not, I do not know, but it seems that way, the way we are talking right now. We are talking about the speeding up of our daily life and the emphasis and the value placed upon that speeding up. You could also see lots of other things taking place in the world, but the value is not on slowness, the value is on speed. A quick child means an intelligent child, a bright child. It is inherent in the very idea of the Enlightenment, of turning against darkness. The values that we ensconce as the higher ones seem to be more manic than depressive, more martial than melancholy. Or really "choleric" rather than "melancholic," to use the old language. I am trying to make a distinction between the values and the observations.

---

5. See James Hillman, *A Terrible Love of War* (New York: Penguin Press, 2004), 209: "I recall hearing Aldous Huxley remark that moderns have been able to add only one sin to the traditional Seven Deadlies: Haste."

Quickness is one of the supposed signs of intelligence. Which would make the ferret smarter than the elephant, or smarter than the oyster certainly. And oysters have been around for fifty million years without ever having had to change anything! So I think they are pretty smart. But we measure intelligence partly by quickness. We have a mercurial idea of intelligence. The very word "slow" in our language means someone who is intellectually disabled. It is one of the ways some people talk, "Her child is slow," meaning low intelligence, not up to speed.

Now, to the definition of manic in psychiatry. There are three main points: an elation of feelings, hyperactivity of willing, and flights of thinking. Very, very simple. But one of the nicest definitions is an absence of sadness. Another one is an absence of inwardness.

And it is not about a lack of feeling. There is feeling is there. It is a certain kind of feeling, a euphoric feeling. It is a high, because we cannot identify feeling sadness. It is not "feeling" the way it is used sentimentally about tears or relationship or valentines. It is not that feeling. So there is an absence of sadness, of inwardness—but feeling is not lost, it is affected by this acceleration, this intensity of fury. Some of you are clinicians. Have any of you seen a person in the high, full-blown manic state where the person is usually locked up if possible, because they are throwing themselves at the walls, and they are in the straitjacket because they are so absolutely wild with fury? They do not eat for forty-eight hours. They do not sleep and they are ready to attack anything. That is a full-blown manic state. The curious thing is that in a full-blown manic state, there is no sleeping or eating. There is no sense of even of being in a body except as an instrument of action. Sometimes, manic people, if it goes long enough, collapse from dehydration, exhaustion, and are in danger. They would not feel pain. That is a curious part of the condition—it is not delusional; it is energetic. That is a big difference.

Inwardness gets taken literally, going inside yourself. I do not understand inwardness only that way. I see inwardness as going into anything. Inwardness can be going into a church, which is one of the oldest ways of encountering inwardness. It can be going into a forest, it can be going into a single tree and being with the tree for its inwardness. There is inwardness of many different sorts. It is not only having an active imagination or a dialog with yourself or sitting in a room alone or something. This is very important: that inwardness is not taken so very literally. Inwardness is the pause of considering the inward nature of anything. Now if you think about the place of therapy in a manic society you begin to realize how important therapy becomes. It is the place of inwardness. It is almost a counterculture necessity.

*Manic Defense*

The speeding up of psychic processes has been called by some psychologists—I think it comes from the Kleinians in London—a manic defense.[6] That is, depression is so difficult that individual people—we wo not talk about the culture for now—but individual people find ways of defending themselves against depression by resorting to manic defenses, forms of denial. Increased activity, increased spending. Spending is very important. In a hyper-manic, or in a hypo-manic, sub-manic condition you tend to spend your money freely. You are not only uninhibited sexually but uninhibited regarding your money. Shopping is considered a major passion. I had a case I remember in Zurich, a woman who not only invited into her apartment various delivery people for very brief sex—it had to be fast, of course—but these were the delivery people who were delivering the things that she had bought. So it was all worked very well. She got sort of a double! And she was purchasing very high-powered stuff from jewelry stores on the Bahnhofstrasse. A friend of mine had a manic patient who invited the Vienna Philharmonic, a 106-piece orchestra, to come to his estate in the country—a manic fantasy to bring in the entire Vienna Philharmonic—an extravagance.

Hyperactivity of the will—rushing around and getting a lot done. You keep your schedule packed and when there is any spare time, you shop. The shopping is so terribly important. It is our second largest leisure activity in the US. The first is watching TV, shopping is the second. I was in Minnesota recently and the new mall has just opened there—the largest mall in the United States, and in the world[7]—and there is something very

---

6. See Melanie Klein, "Mourning and its Relation to Manic-Depressive States," *The International Journal of Psychoanalysis* 21 (1940): 125–53; also John Steiner, *Psychic Retreats: Pathological Organizations in Psychotic, Neurotic and Borderline Patients* (London and New York: Routledge, 1993).

7. The Mall of America, which opened in 1992, located in Bloomington, just 15 minutes from downtown Minneapolis and St. Paul.

important in what they have succeeded in doing in this mall. There is a group of psychologically interested people who looked at the mall in order to get at the myth that is going on there and one observation they made is that you become so distracted and so fragmented by the plethora of events that the act of buying something is the only way that you can come back together as a person. You are all over the place and by taking out your credit card and making a purchase you've become a person again. See how effective it is? So going shopping is not necessarily being dissipated. Shopping is a way of finding an identity. So do not worry, the depression will not last long, we will be buying again!

At the moment I am simply describing the mania of the culture. I am not explaining it so I am not using a physiological or psychological explanation, but simply giving a description. It is to open our eyes to what we consider to be normal life, normal TV life, business life, shopping life, eating life, and to show that our normal culture favors a manic way of behavior. Were you to come in from another culture where people sit around a lot, where people are late, where people get up late, where people hang out, where people do not do much, sell a few peanuts, it is a completely different way of living a day.

Within our culture, the psyche is silence is forbidden. TV dominates our way of life and the worst thing that can happen is for there to be a moment of silence, because viewers—fourteen million of them—might switch off and change channels. The thing must keep moving. Think about the meaning a cell phone for someone stuck in traffic, which is a depressive isolating moment. So it is like a handheld remedy for the thruway that is no longer going through anywhere. See how difficult it is for any single person to have a moment, a month, six months of depression in this situation, how difficult it is? In one of my books I said something about the revolution begins with standing in, standing for your own depression, then you are really revolting against the society, against the society's pace and rhythm.[8]

---

8. James Hillman, *Re-Visioning Psychology* (New York: Harper & Row, 1975), 98–99: *"The true revolution begins in the individual who can be true to his or her depression.* Neither jerking oneself out of it, caught in cycles of hype and despair, nor suffering it through till it turns, nor theologizing it—but discovering the consciousness and depths it wants. So begins the revolution in behalf of soul."

Now if we look at how the bonuses are paid in the big corporations and the way the life is lived, is it so different? Diagnostically, is it so different from what we have been describing? It is acceptable. It fits within the whole pattern. We do not regard it as manic, as exaggerated, as a defense against depression, a manic defense. There is a social aspect to this all along. These are not just conditions that you and I suffer from or indulge in, they are part of the way our civilization, our American contemporary civilization, lives. Now the one thing we do know psychiatrically is that the manic condition can collapse suddenly. And that anxiety dominates Mr. Greenspan.[9] That at any moment this whole thing could go down the tubes. And so we see pictures every now and then on TV about the horrors of the 1930s: people selling apples and the soup kitchens and the bread lines and so on, forgetting that already in the civilization that we are living in, one fifth of the population is already there and has been going down lower, and another two fifths are not in that manic part. But they are in the manic part in the attempt to keep up the pace. So people will have two and three jobs, and nobody's home with the kids. It is the whole story that you all are familiar with. But we can tie this all together with this devotion to what the Kleinians call a manic defense.

That feeling of being in a manic condition—you can transpose it to the entire civilization—it is an exhausting experience of not being able to catch all that rushes through your head. You cannot write it down, you cannot speak it out. The associational pathways are going in all directions, one word leads to another, one thought leads to another. There is a kind of verbal speed, or what is called a *logorrhea*, diarrhea of the logos. People keep voluminous journals and notebooks, delusional systems begin to develop, words lead to other words. That is not paranoid delusional or schizophrenic delusional, mixed up speech, but a pressure is felt to get it all out and get it all down and keep up with the way that it is moving in your own psyche. There is a sense of erotic power and a sense of phallic power. Of sexual potency. And, in fact, the money complexes are where both mania and depression strike. Depression makes you feel tenuous, broke, that you are going to end up as a bag lady, and the manic condition makes you feel wealthy to the world. Quantities and numbers

---

9. Alan Greenspan was Chairman of the United States Federal Reserve Board from 1987 to 2006.

play a role in this. And it is again interesting to notice, if we imagine our economy, imagine our lives in quantities and numbers—billions and trillions, extraordinary numbers I do not know how to write them down, a trillion—how many zeros laid out? And, of course, the fascination with space and the enormous distances. These, too, are, in a way, a kind of manic fantasy because the earth makes us sad. The earth brings sadness with it. Space does not. Have you ever seen a sad *Star Trek* episode? It is all visions, future, and those fantastic rockets going off.

We are involved in a rhetoric of speed, and we should see this manic condition or this hyper-manic civilization not in terms of the content, but in terms of the mood and speed. Thinking is faster, activity is faster, and feeling is faster or higher. It belongs to what was called in the Renaissance or even earlier, the rhetoric of speed, or *celeritas*—rapidity. And interestingly, this word, *celeritas*, has the same root as the word *celebrity*. So the celebrity culture and fast fame is part of the same rhetoric—the manic rhetoric. Now what is so strange is that these values dominate so much of what we do and so much of the way we think we should be living. They dominate the dosages we take to keep us up, because you do feel, if you go down, that you are left behind and left out. You are no longer in the race or in the swim. And this is so difficult for any individual who has a pause, who cannot keep up, that you do imagine and feel yourself not sad but crazy. Diagnostically sick because you are not in the swim any longer.

So we do not know what happens when we fall out. The dread is that we might fall out. If we do not keep up, we will fall out, that is the formula, whereas we are not certain what will happen if we fall out. You see what I mean? It is not a necessity that if you fall out you are going to die. But it feels that way especially if you are overmortgaged, which is part of the manic condition. Do you see how that fits in? You take on more debt—we have huge consumer debt right now, huge!—so we have to keep up our payments and so on.

What memory is there in this acceleration, this *celeritas*? High speed movement. Think of a high speed train going through the landscape—what do you see out the window? Where is the memory? Memory is something that pulls you back and down and in. So memorial ceremonies and memorial moments in the culture are very important.

Which came first, the manic desire in the culture, in the civilization, that has to move forward and the technological progress that facilitates it or is the technology its own devil's apprentice that moves the culture forward? They seem to go hand in hand. Media accelerates consciousness, and consciousness demands acceleration.

Now, I have not used the word pathological yet. I am rather in the world of description and trying to place depression in a manic civilization. Because if we only talk about depression, we are forgetting the context in which we are depressed. And the context needs to be examined. I do not have an idea of when this sped-up thing began and how far it should go. Maybe we should all think that we are still not there yet, that we can go a lot faster than we are going possibly, but we may lose more and more people falling off the train as we move forward. I mean that is the point of asking "How do you keep up?" If the new cyberworld is run by people in their twenties, as the new day traders are in their twenties, it may just get younger and younger and maybe we are not there yet. We may find that the kids on their various machines are where we are going and that they are way ahead of us.

The fact is that the United States happens to be top dog on the world level, and everybody wants to be like us, to do the same thing. But that is only the first level of explanation. I believe there is a little more to it than that. It is seductive. We ought to get a hold of that and think about that. Why is it so attractive? A person who is on the go, who is with it, who is moving, he can go all day long, the type-A, alpha animal, and all the equipment that goes with that which hastens: he can be on two lines at once, talk to three people at once, or do six things at once, and so on. That, as well as the technical equipment, is very attractive to other people because, perhaps, it relieves the innate sadness of being on the earth. Perhaps. It seems to offer joy, euphoria, exhilaration.

Triumph is certainly part of the manic feeling. But it is a little more subtle than that. It is not just triumph, because triumph tends to mean victory, and that stops. But there is a *sentiment de plénitude* there too. A feeling that I have not been able to get it all, that there is still more to do, still more thought pouring into my head, still more to buy, 6,000 windows to put in. The triumph is never achieved, the pressure is tremendous. One of the images used in psychiatry for mania is a too-narrow tube through which an enormous amount of water is rushing, so the pressure, the sense of inward pressure, is enormous. That forces the activities. Whereas in the depressed state it is the feeling of it going out everywhere and nowhere, no direction, no pressure, a feeling of sinking. And this manic pressure feels good—there is an elation of feeling—euphoria—but what does it do to others? You may feel good, but what about others? That is a huge question. And what does it do, if we accept the notion of soul, to the soul, even if you are feeling good?

The manic feeling is that time is moving like a river very quickly and you have to stay in that, if you are not in that, life passes you by. Now that is not a depressive feeling of time where time stands still and one can drop deeper and deeper and deeper into time, into this moment, into stillness or silence. Then this river rushing by is just white noise and you can get back in at any point. But when you are in the river, the feeling is entirely different. The stones at the bottom of the river do not move much, but they make the river adjust to the way the stone is.

*Melancholy*

Where then is the depression, if mania and depression are so often thought as of belonging together? If they are thought of belonging together, whether physiologically in the bi-polar circular disorder, or as yin and yang, or as up and down, and so on, then where is the other part in a manic culture? That is what the soul again and again feels in each of us, what the soul drops into, and is miserable because of. We who are on top find that depression is the dominant symptom in the culture. Its the number one symptom in the culture, in this on-top manic culture. And where does it fall most of the time, according to the statistics on the presentation of odd complaints to physicians? It falls mainly on women. Women carry the depression for our culture. This is true for England also. I do not know about Germany and Sweden, and so on. In England—I do not know the statistics here maybe some of you do—15 to 20 percent of hospital admissions, not just mental hospital admission, are for mental depression, and of those, 75 percent are women. There is something about the culture that loads the women with depression. Or there is something about women that makes them able to receive the depression, however you want to put it. Or there is something that does not happen to men as often that happens to women. Or there is something that men are able to conceal through cultural support, who knows?

In recent years there have been more and more new descriptions of depression in teenagers and in childhood and a large increase in children's suicide. So where is the depression when the culture is dedicated to the manic condition? It falls first on women, and second on children. And now with feminism refusing the depression that has fallen on them from this kind of culture, it seems it falls ever so much more on children. I think it also exacerbates the natural sadness that is in the world. Robert Bly talks about the sadness that is in nature.[10] Gestalt psychology talks about it in another language: the face of the landscape, certain cloudscapes, certain sea scenes, forest scenes that are sad. They are not projections from my mind on that forest scene or seascape, but the qualities of form in the seascape are in themselves sad just as they might be joyful.

Now if we are not carrying the depressive side, the Saturnian side, whatever we call it, then where is it? In women and children yes, but it will become exaggerated elsewhere I would think and I would think nature and the outer world, the object world, becomes sadder and sadder and looks more and more depressed. Things begin to fall apart, they look disheveled, neglected, crappy, cheap, miserable, homeless. Not just people. The world has become homeless. And so your sense that you become more and more depressed, in that environment of LA, is partly the neglect of the melancholy of the world and the exacerbation of the melancholy. Because I am assuming that melancholy is a given to the planet and it needs to be cared for. And if melancholy is not cared for it becomes clinical depression.

Melancholy is the larger term which has become secularized and reduced and clinicized into a thing called depression. Since it is a neglected god, and, as Jung says, the gods have become diseases,[11] the neglected god of melancholy becomes clinical depression. So the job before us is to revert depression back to melancholy. Not to cure depression, not to lick depression and make us happy like the Declaration of Independence

---

10. *News of the Universe: Poems of Twofold Consciousness*, chosen and introduced by Robert Bly (Berkeley: Counterpoint, 1995), 9.

11. C.G. Jung, *CW* 13: 54.

says we should be, but to increase our understanding of and capacity for melancholy.

There is something demographic in the culture that we should think about in regard to the place depression has in it. The culture is becoming more a senex culture, an older culture demographically. Now of the major powers, we have got the oldest democratic system. I mean the Swiss have theirs, but ours has lasted over 200 years. But what is important is the demographics, and that the aging population is living longer. We are moving more and more into an aging population. Were it not for the immigration to this country our population would be much older demographically. We have a habit of looking back on the golden days, and this belongs to a senex culture. Whether we look back on Reagan's golden days or Reagan looks back on his golden days, there is nostalgia for the golden days and a recapitulating of the past. There is a hatred of youth and children. A hatred of youth and children—I will argue that one a long time if you want to argue with me. The neglect, the abuse: it is extraordinary. I mean, one out of seven children in America is hungry and now we are going to cut their breakfast out too. The feelings of gridlock, of stasis, of corruption, of blocking, of pollution, of toxicity, of refuse, wastage, these constant preoccupations with this whether it is in ourselves or in the media or wherever—these are new imaginations in the culture compared to what was in the imagination of the culture fifty years ago. It was forward looking, there was a feeling that everything's possible. Now there is a feeling that things are not possible in the same way, and that restriction is the way to go—cutting back, closing down, shutting off, sunsetting. These are all senex fantasies. So this has something to do with depression coming into our culture in some different way than it has before. At the same time, there is a lot of resistance to the role of depression. For example, if you are in an office you do not want to be the heavy, you do not want to be the one who lays out the laws, who has to fire people, who has to set up structures. The very word, the heavy, to be the heavy in the office or in the system or in the health unit or wherever... avoiding this is part of not wanting to assume this kind of place. You should be light and easy and friendly and connected and so on. Lighten up! But to be the heavy is an aspect of the melancholic part of you, and is able to maintain that position.

*Economics and Psyche*

There is also a parallel in our culture between economics and psychiatry. The word "depression" is an economic term today, as are endless numbers of words that have been appropriated from the psyche by economics: credit, interest, trust, bond, obligation, yield, safe, security—you can go on for twenty, thirty terms that are the basic language of human relationships that have been appropriated by economics as part of this tremendous expansion of the economic mind over the other kinds of mind. And the economic mind is terribly afraid of depression. During that period in the 1980s, I think '81 or '82, when the word recession was used again and again—severe recession, deep recession—they would never get to depression.

In economics, one of the signs of depression is a low construction rate and a decline in home building, and in psychiatry, one of the feelings of depression is no future. In psychiatry the description of depression includes an inhibition of drive. In economics you get driving restrictions: energy crises, small cars, no gas. The things we had in 1973. In psychiatry, you have a lowering or loss of libido, and in economics, you get fantasies of the exhaustion of the reserve, of raw materials, fossil fuels. In economics there are all sorts of ideas of doom that programs like Medicare will fail, that Social Security will go bankrupt, that there will be rampant unemployment. And in depression, you cannot work, you cannot concentrate. These projections of the future are sociologically and economically parallel with the same kind of doom fantasies of the future that you get in the psychiatric descriptions of the depressive condition. And in economics, you put blame on the past and leave a debt to the children. You blame the past: they did it wrong; they fucked up, they screwed up; the former administration, the bankers, the former laws, the Smoot-Hawley Tariff Act of 1930 brought on the depression. This blaming of the past is exactly what goes on in the psychiatric form of depression. It is the remorse, looking backward and seeing blackness in the past, having done things wrong. So there is a parallel all the way through and a lot of the language we read in the papers about depression or about the doom that is coming or what is wrong with the future is language that is the same language that belongs to the psychiatry of an individual. We have to read doom forecasts as archetypal expressions of Saturn because the same think tank can also work up a strategy for an extraordinary future. There are two forecasts, for example, about LA right now. One says that it will disintegrate into a total chaotic disaster and the other sees possibilities for all sorts of wonderful things. These various forecasts are projections as they say, they even use the same word: projections. So we have to read these projections psychologically. What archetype is speaking in this or that projection?

Also interesting—and we will come to this later—is Karl Marx's fantasy that capitalism will produce a huge depression, that it cannot go on, that it will collapse, and that capitalism can only be rescued by war. The Marxists claim that is exactly how Roosevelt ended the depression of the 1930s, that it was only resolved by the war of 1940. That was the Marxist view. Now that view, that the only way out of the Saturnian condition is a martial one, reappears in psychiatry with the violent treatments of depression. So there are parallels all the way through between the economics or the politics and the psychology of individual cases. These are brought out by what I would call archetypal thinking.

I suppose I should take back a few things. One, of course, is that everything that moves fast is not necessarily bad. If that were the case, hawks would never eat. Or I would never have been able to get here so quickly, and so on. It is also important to realize that it is in relation to depression that I am talking about speed. Not all speed is bad. One of our troubles of being Americans is that we are brought up as moralists. We always think in terms of good and bad before we think in terms of anything else. Before we look at a phenomenon, we want to know "Is it good or bad?," and this gets in the way of everything. We do not ask questions like "Which way is it going?," "How big is it?," "What color is it?," or "What does it smell like?" We want to begin with "Is it good or bad?," "Did I have a good dream or a bad dream?"—rather than "What was the dream?" The fact is you cannot tell what is good or bad in psychic events very easily. Because starting with this question of "good or bad" means that we are beginning to condemn everything accelerated and that is not really the point. The point is to be descriptive rather than moralistic.

And also it is important to understand there is a distinction between what might be called a puer flight and mania. That is, the young man with wings, the youthful fire of Hermes or Eros that flies, that is inspired, that is intuitive and idealistic, is not manic. So just because your boyfriend gets flashes of ideas and has set up this and that new computer company does not necessarily mean that he is in a manic state. This belongs with puer inspiration. So one needs to spend time looking at things before deciding diagnostically where they belong.

*The Depressive Syndrome*

Now to the subject of the depressive syndrome. It should really be "In Defense of Depression," but it would not sound as clinical as "The Depressive Syndrome," right? "Syndrome" is a very good word because syndrome implies lots of different things running together. To deal with a syndrome, you need a cultural approach because the amount of things that are running together: *syn* plus *drome.*

We are going to be exploring some of the language of melancholy. What we have so far is only the language of depression and so we need to begin to be able to open up to the language of melancholy. We are in the area of mood. We are in the mood of beauty, and of longing and nostalgia, sadness, and despair.

Now, to be clear, I think there are depressions in all cultures. I think there are different qualities and different focuses,, and different feelings of depression. It may transcend the cultural dimension with different contents in different cultures. Just as all cultures have some notion of "crazy," but what they declare "crazy" will differ from culture to culture. But "crazy" is an archetypal or universal quality. What is important here is what matters for us, how it feels for us in our particular culture. And words matter, and if we call this thing melancholy it has one kind of feeling and if we call it depression it has another kind of feeling.

You know, a psychologist in the early part of this century did an index of words for feelings and he had 1,500 words for different feelings all within our ordinary English language. Somehow we have lost a lot of the richness of description. You can use of the body for mimicry to get back some of that. How do you feel when your hand is there and you are standing like that? Do you feel independent? Do you feel aggressive? Do you feel tough? Do you feel safe? There is an enormous range of feeling that we can get to through that body language.

The best way to get to the archetypal is through feeling, not through definition. The mistake that most people make about the archetypal is to treat it as a noun and to try to define it. And I have said this again and again: it is an *adjective*—it qualifies events. As an adjective, it becomes something you feel. I think we need very much to differentiate the range of emotion that is covered with this general word depression. For example, depression is a secular term for melancholy, and in that sense it leaves out a great deal—as a term.

I cannot claim to be a melancholic personality. I cannot claim to be a Saturnian type, but I notice when I go back in my own history that I keep coming to the same places, the same rocks again and again. I wrote a whole book on suicide. I wrote a book on the underworld, Hades, and death.[12] I wrote back in the 1960s on betrayal,[13] and on the Senex and Saturn.[14] I did a whole piece on paranoia,[15] and a whole piece on necessity.[16] These are all part of the melancholic strand of life so that even though I cannot claim the joys and pleasures of being a melancholic as a personality, I have nonetheless some brute level that is melancholic or a strand of lead that is heavy in my psyche and I am drawn again and again to this topic.

Today this topic is hot. The government itself is very interested in it. And when we get to the politics we will talk about that. It is almost as if we have discovered depression, finally, in the United States. Now I have to apologize for perhaps being not as profound as some of you in the audience who are melancholic by nature, or as profound as some of the patients you may have to deal with and work with, or live with, people in your own household, or families. But I also feel because of this countercurrent in my own nature I can connect with it somehow.

One of the people that I learned something from, now dead—it is very important to keep referring to the dead not only in this subject but any

---

12. *The Dream and the Underworld* (New York: Harper & Row, 1979).

13. "Betrayal," *The Guild of Pastoral Psychology,* Guild Lecture No. 128 (London, 1964); reprinted in *UE* 3: *Senex & Puer.*

14. "On Senex Consciousness," *Spring: An Annual of Archetypal Psychology and Jungian Thought* (1970); reprinted in *UE* 3: *Senex & Puer.*

15. *On Paranoia,* Eranos Lectures Series, vol. 8 (Dallas: Spring Publications, 1988); reprinted in *UE* 7: *Inhuman Relations.*

16. "On the Necessity of Abnormal Psychology," *Eranos Yearbook* 43 (1974); reprinted as "Athene, Ananke, and the Necessity of Abnormal Psychology" in *UE* 6: *Mythic Figures.*

subject—was John Layard, an English anthropologist and Jungian analyst. Layard wrote a remarkable book of anthropology in the early part of the twentieth century called *Stone Men of Malakula*, and then he did some Eranos lectures and wrote two papers on the virgin archetype.[17] He used to make these remarks when he was talking or hanging out or whatever, one of them was that "depression is withheld knowledge." I wrote that down years ago. I never understood what he was talking about. I usually did not get what he was talking about. But I think what we will be doing here is working on *withheld knowledge*. There is withheld knowledge in depression that is masked and lost by our diagnostics and our resistance to it. Withheld knowledge. In other words, we have to put depression somehow in an archetypal context in order to get back to the knowledge that could be withheld not only by us, but by depression's silence, or muteness, and also the culture which resists the interest in it and the investigation of it.

I think that you could say either way that depression results in withheld knowledge—the silence, the mutism—or that knowledge is not coming through. But that there is something in the depression that knows something and the depression withholds it. There is something that knows something. Now that is a very basic psychotherapeutic idea, that there is something in the symptom that knows something. That is what Jung calls the consciousness in the symptom. It is why Freud thought repression is so bad, because there are repressed ideas, repressed contents, and things are being withheld. Two ways: depression as knowing something we would prefer not to know. Something not appearing—a knowledge withheld—not withheld because it is repressed but because it is distonic to the ego's way of living. We would prefer not to know. And also something repressed.

*Therapy as Depressive Activity*

In the Renaissance, in the late 1500s, one of the descriptions of the manic and the melancholic was in terms of sadness. The melancholic had fixed

---

17. John Layard, *Stone Men of Malekula: Vao* (London: Chatto & Windus, 1942); *The Virgin Archetype: Two Papers* (Zurich: Spring Publications, 1972); *Celtic Quest: Sexuality and Soul in Individuation—A Depth-Psychology Study of the Mabinogion Legend of Culhwch and Olwen* (Zurich: Spring Publications, 1975).

ideas, but they were qualified by sadness. And in the manic there was an absence of sadness. So we begin to get hold of two things: inwardness and sadness that are absent from the manic condition, inwardness and sadness that become crucial parts of the melancholic temperament and the melancholic condition. I mentioned before that therapy becomes a place and a refuge for inwardness and sadness in a manic society. Therapy as psychotherapy. And we have to see that psychotherapy is really a depressive activity. And if one does not have a connection to the melancholic part of the soul, the melancholic temperament, doing therapy is not going to be easy. The patient that one works with needs to understand that everything—or a great deal of what we do in therapy—constellates melancholy. The emphasis on time, the knowledge that it takes a long time, this goes back to Freud. You had to sign up for three years and you had to meet regularly. This "chronicity" is important. Chronos is another name for the god Saturn. We are talking about what the alchemists called the *longissima via*—the longest way. Therapy proceeds by the longest routes, there are no short cuts. So the whole notion of managed care, crisis intervention run by the insurance companies so that you meet for six times only and then you have to show why you can go on with it—all these short cuts do not belong to the melancholy aspect of therapy; they are an adaptation of therapy to the manic condition.

One of Freud's main ideas, in the early years of psychotherapy in Vienna, was that when you enter into the psychoanalytic contract, and this contractual arrangement was carried out by the Freudians, you would show up for fifty weeks a year, both of you would take your vacation at the same time, and the future was on hold. You would make no changes in your life—not change your job, or spouse, or your place of residence. You would maintain what you were and you would stay in that condition and that was the container, so to speak, for the work. The future was in suspension. And in fact, changes that began to go into the world were considered acting out. So there is a very Saturnian sense of stasis within which the psychodynamics unfold.

Therapy has this depressive component of sameness. Let us just think of all the things that go on in therapy. Coming to the same place, to the same office, often at the same time, for regular visits, is in itself a repetition. It has a depressive quality to it. Going back over the past, looking back, whether it is resentment, remorse, repentance, regret, resistance, the whole set of "re's" you spend your time with in psychotherapy, are part of the turning backward and inward that belongs to Saturn and melancholy. And also the incredible slowness that goes with it. The slowness of insights—you get an insight and then it is gone. You get a flash, something interesting, and then you have to get the same insight again and again and again for it to take. The preoccupation with the wrong, with what went wrong, what is wrong with me, with my complaint, the sense of a complaint, the sense of being wrong or the world being wrong, and working on one's wrongs and how one has wronged others and so on and so forth. This belongs also to the melancholy feeling, because when you are in a depression very much of your attention is on what is wrong.

If the society lives in a denial of depression, if we take this manic condition as a denial of depression, then the question is, why does it spread through the world? And the reply is that it is more pleasant to feel that than depression—putting it into the pain-pleasure rule of how human behavior works. We need to understand that, whatever we want to call it, denial of pain, denial of sadness, denial of inwardness, there is some kind of denial. There does not seem to be any defense against this denial even in the Buddhist cultures that understand these things. The Buddhist cultures also fall victim to hamburgers, fast food, the whole manic thing. We in America who go Buddhist, we may be holier than the Buddhists who live in Thailand, you know. That is, more Protestant about it. I do not know the worldwide answer. I am concerned with bringing an awareness to people engaged in therapy of the inherent saturnine or melancholic aspect of therapy. It should not be a surprise that your patients and you are depressed in therapy. And that burnout comes, I think, from not having that chronic sense that goes with therapy. One goes into a chronic situation with an acute fantasy. In other words, you are going into it with the idea of a fever rather than a long-term scoliosis or something that is structural in the bones. The more you can go at it with the melancholy aspect of your nature, the more tolerance there is for what goes on. Slowness is part of the work.

Jung talks about this a lot in his writings about therapy, especially when he writes about alchemy and therapy. Here are some of the qualities of therapeutic work that are not manic. One is the negative irony that goes on in therapy. There is a wry smile that goes on in therapy, those recognitions that taste of the bitter, bitter truths. There is a beauty in those kinds of moments. Now that is the beauty that goes with melancholy. There is a kind of what one writer has called a lugubrious energy in therapy. Not an elated energy but an energy of heaviness. You can feel the difference when you come in off the street and get in the therapist's office. There is a different energy in the room—an expectation of heaviness. And an expectation of something dismal. It is like going into a dark forest, a swamp, or a bog, and the language gets tortuous and repetitious, and it so rarely flares into something quick and witty. Julia Kristeva, one of the feminist Freudians, a Bulgarian woman who writes in French and a major figure in the Freudian, feminist thinking in Paris, writes: "Without a bent for melancholia, there is no psyche, only a transition to act or play."[18] Now that is a heavy statement. I have heard other therapists say that therapy only begins when a patient starts to be depressed. It cannot begin before that. In alchemy, the *nigredo* is an accomplishment. The blackening of the work is an accomplishment. It is a stage, but not a beginning stage. The patient, the stone, the work is already full of other kinds of fantasies—it wants to get better, wants to get a job, wants to get married, wants to meet somebody significant. It wants something to happen. It is only when that turns black—the whole thing blackens—that the therapy begins, as at the end of *Portnoy's Complaint.* "Now vee may perhaps to begin. Yes?"[19] says the therapist at the end of the novel, after all the insane acting out is over. Now this is classic. I am not saying that this is the way it has to be or that there are not new ideas about therapy today regarding the world, and rethinking the notions of acting out. I only want to point out this aspect of therapy since that is where we are in our discussion of the melancholic inspiration of therapy.

"Without a bent for melancholia, there is no psyche" (others would say there is no soul), "only a transition to act or play." They are just playing a game. They have not been affected, caught; the torture has not begun. Now one of the reasons for this is that, in the writings of the

---

18. Julia Kristeva, *Black Sun: Depression and Melancolia,* translated by Leon S. Roudiez (New York: Columbia University Press, 1989), 4.

19. Philip Roth, *Portnoy's Complaint* (New York: Random House, 1969), 274.

Renaissance or even the alchemists as far back as Albertus Magnus, the melancholic fantasies, the obfuscation, and the darkness and oppression produce a state of pensiveness. That is, reflecting, pondering, weighing, considering, which has as its end goal *contemplation* and was a great virtue in the Middle Ages and the Renaissance. Giulio Camillo claimed that Man "cannot contemplate unless he becomes pensive."[20] You cannot really think a thought in the manic condition, because you may have ideas, or even a flight of ideas, but you do not *think* the ideas. There is a great deal of difference between having an idea and thinking an idea. Thinking is a lot of work and it is slow. Ideas, they just come when they come. And again the Renaissance liked melancholy so much and most of them considered themselves melancholic, including Michelangelo and Ficino. The idea was that you could not become a contemplative, you could not really philosophize, you could not really understand the world or relate to God or "find the self" in today's language unless you become pensive. And you do not become pensive voluntarily—you either become pensive through your nature, that is, through your melancholic temperament, or you are driven to pensiveness by what we would call depression.

I think right here I should say that we have to be careful, since this is our theme—the depressive or the melancholic—not to erode the categories and say that this is *the* great thing. Because two years from now we will be talking about another syndrome, and then we will say that *this* is the great thing. Like paranoia. It is not that. You can also do extraordinary puer creative things like that! Snap! You can cook up a rap piece without any time and without any repetition and just rap. So I do not want to say that it is necessary. It is necessary for a *certain kind of soul work*, but I would not want to say that it is the whole bag of creativity.

Therapy itself is a pathological phenomenon. I mean that we have to have this strange activity. There is such a thing as sitting still, sitting with it, and contemplate—but in the classical work, that was always a provenance of Saturn, of contemplation, pensiveness, pondering, and it is this quality of time, pausing, that you bring with it. In music it is called a rest.

---

20. *Nuovo Libro di Lettere de i piu rari auttori della lingua volgare italiana, di nuovo, et con nuovo additione ristampato,* edited by Paolo Gherardo (Venice, 1545), 70.

You do not get the beauty unless you get the slowness—slowness is essential. There is a terrible absence of beauty in the culture. The difficulty we have with beauty is partly because we do not have the slowness to receive it. The making of beauty requires certain depressive activities like repetition, lingering, dwelling. Henry James called writing a novel "a prolonged hovering flight of the subjective over the outstretched case exposed."[21] Just being over it for this long, slow time.

Lingering in front of a painting does not mean that you have to be sad looking at the thing. I do not mean that. I mean that when you are standing there in front of a painting, there has to be a dropping in and a slowing down to see it. Wouldn't you think so? I am putting that lingering in with a certain slowing down of one's entire habits of life. Looking again and again, seeing more in it, feeling more through it. It is not that paintings have to be sad like Rembrandt's self-portrait—but there is something in the arts or beauty that requires a slowing down.

When Jung describes some of the nature of what he called the mercurial substance of the whole work, that is, the nature of the psyche itself, it is comprised of ominous substances: "*succus lunariae* or *lunatica* (juice of the moon-plant), aqua Saturni..., poison, scorpion, dragon, boys' or dogs' urine, brimstone, devil."[22] Another passage from someone else, not Jung, mentions feces, menstrual blood, dung. It has all these materials at the beginning of the work. And the German alchemist Michael Maier said that the journey, the process of the work, which I would call therapeutic work, begins in lead and ends in lead.[23] Now it is easy enough to understand that it begins in lead, that it is only when you are really heavy with what is wrong and you being wrong, that examination of past and self and so on will begin. But why does it end in lead? What is that lead that it ends in?

Marvin Spiegelman, who is an analyst in Los Angeles, edited a book called *Jungian Analysts: Their Visions and Vulnerabilities*.[24] He writes that

---

21. "The New Novel," in Henry James, *Selected Literary Criticism*, edited by Morris Shapira (London, Melbourne, and Toronto: Heinemann, 1963), 333.

22. *CW* 16: 408.

23. *Atalanta fugiens* (1618), online at *https://furnaceandfugue.org*.

24. *Jungian Analysts: Their Visions and Vulnerabilities*, edited by J. Marvin Spiegelman (Phoenix: New Falcon Publications, 1988).

depression is the most typical and frequent form of psychopathology found among Jungian analysts. I would think that is not surprising—not because they are Jungians, and not because they are analysts, but because depression is the major syndrome of our culture. It is what presents itself most in the consulting room of physicians, and ministers, and social workers—those who are in the helping professions, not just in the consulting rooms of the psychiatrists and psychoanalysts, but those people who are in the front lines of the helping professions. The major syndrome of our Western culture—not just the United States, but England, Germany, and Switzerland, which are the only countries I know—is what is called depression. So why would it not be the most typical and frequent form of psychopathology found among analysts? In other words, what we are now discovering is that this is the dominant wrongness in the citizen. The citizen suffers depression. We can see that what is called depression, the qualities that characterize depression, have a difficult time in this civilization. Which means that our own moments of depression are very difficult for us, more difficult than some of the other problems that we may have. But therapy feels the importance of depression. For instance, Donald Meltzer says, "to be done well, it must 'hurt.' "[25] It must be done under great strains. Freud has this great sentence: "Much will be gained if we succeed in transforming your hysterical misery into common unhappiness."[26] That is from his *Studies on Hysteria.* And Jung says of the aim of psychotherapy: "*The patient has not to learn how to get rid of his neurosis but how to bear it.*"[27] And that is what I think he means by inauthentic and authentic suffering. Inauthentic suffering becomes neurotic and difficult to bear and forced on other people to bear as well—your partner, your mother, your son. And *eigentliches* or authentic suffering, that is, the suffering that is part of your fate, your karma or dharma, Moira or Themis or whatever—belongs to you and you must learn to bear it. And that is what

25. "Psychoanalysis as a Human Activity," in *Selected Papers of Donald Meltzer,* vol. 3: *The Psychoanalytic Process and the Analyst,* edited by Meg Harris Williams (London: The Harris Meltzer Trust, 2021), 19.

26. Josef Breuer and Sigmund Freud, *Studies on Hysteria,* translated by James Strachey (New York: Basic Books, 1957), 305.

27. *CW*10: 360.

therapy does. It moves you from the unbearable, meaning what you are not bearing, to what is bearable.

One of the reasons that therapy invites melancholia or is a practice in melancholia, has to do with loss. There is an essential necessity for the loss of the literal world, or the death of the literal world, in order to uncover the psychic reality. In other words, it is only when you are able to lose or go through the loss of the things you cling to as real, that psychic reality becomes more important. All you have left is your psychic reality. Your dreams, your images, your feelings, your memories, and being able to see through those or deliteralize them. And that seems to be one of the purposes of melancholy.

As we begin to get into melancholy as we are now, the room quiets, there is not as many hands up, not many who want to talk, the whole thing changes its tone a bit. We are also having a bit of sunset. A decline of the light. I also talk more slowly—not worried about boredom, because when you are depressed you are not worried about boring anyone, you are worried about whether you can even say the next word. There is a drying up and a drying out that happens. Voice gets more monotone. You lose your thread. Now the manic does not lose the thread—it hops from thread to thread. It works by association, by distractibility. See, I am talking along here. My eye catches the microphone, and I begin to jump to that and say something from there, and so on. Whereas with depression you cannot get off the same thing, it is very repetitious. And remember, whereas in the manic condition all things are tinged with the feeling of elation, in depression all things are tinged with psychic pain. So any fantasies about getting better are also tinged with psychic pains. That is one of the cruel paradoxes of depressive treatments—it will only get worse.

Back to the actualities of therapy. I mentioned the regularity of time as part of the Saturnian or melancholic aspect. I mentioned that question that the therapist asks, What's wrong? In German they say, *Was fehlt?* What is missing? What is lacking? Then there is the whole business of the waiting room—I do not know who has waiting rooms any more—people rush in now. In New York, they have a new way of doing therapy—you may have read this already—two women realized that their practices were falling off and partly they were losing patients because the patients were so busy they could not get from their offices to the practice room. They may be working on Wall Street, and the practice room was in the Upper 80s. It is a long way from Wall Street to the Upper 80s, and there is traffic, subways, and taxis, and their patients would miss their hours or cancel them, so it was very difficult. So these women decided they were going to provide a service. They hired a van, they put two chairs in the van and a little table, a box of Kleenex, a little bowl of flowers on the table, and they pick the patient up at the patient's office and drive the patient to their next appointment wherever it is and during the drive, in the van, for 40 minutes they do their therapy on wheels. Like Meals on Wheels, they have this Therapy on Wheels. So no time is lost. It keeps moving. And the appointments are regular. The therapist does not drive the van, the therapist hires a driver, and according to the report it is very hard on the therapist because they have to keep track of the time, of the driver, of the route the driver chooses, the patient's next appointment, and this gives the therapist additional worries. But at least they have a patient!

The waiting room is archetypally the area outside of the *Asclepieion*, the healing temple in ancient Greece where you went before you could go in to sleep and have your dream. In the ancient healing cults, you had to lie on a *kliné*, from which we have the word "clinic"—a kind of couch or bench or stone. I slept on one of those once to have a dream, it was not too successful. So you are in a waiting area, on hold, and then you get to go inside the room for therapy. Now the waiting room is a depressive place, no matter what the magazines are. And waiting is a melancholic psychic activity. Then when you get into the room, you sit or you lie. And those are positions of depression. And then comes the low voice, the little talk, the mutism of the therapist. At least, originally, the therapist was supposed to speak very little. Going back into the case history. The future is in suspension. Any talk about what is coming next is a projection. Change itself, change in the world itself, in classical analysis, is held in suspension until the therapy is over.

With the idea of the presenting a *complaint*, we are also asking for the melancholic, because the word comes from the Latin *plangerer*, beating the breast, striking the breast. So complaint comes with *lament*, to lament with, to grieve with, to share this *mea culpa*, my misery. The initial complaint in the first hour has to do with opening the chest—plaintive sounds—plaintive cries. Complaint is not merely, "My husband and I do not talk to each other anymore." It is a deeply felt complaint of the soul and a feeling that something is lost. So right off the bat, asking for the complaint, whether in medicine or psychotherapy, you are inviting in the depressive element.

Also one of the things you do in therapy is reduce—there is a reduction going on. There is a reductive aspect to looking at the past, at your commonality, and with it comes the realization that you are just one of many people submitting to therapy with the same troubles that everybody else has. That is a very depressive thought, when you realize you are just one more case of someone having trouble with his wife or trouble with her husband. There is an ordinariness and commonality about it despite all the glamorous words like "creative discovery of the self."

Something else I want to mention—I do not know if you will agree with this—I think the attention to images is depressive too. The attention to a dream, the attention to a single image, looking at a painting, regardless of its subject, there is something about the framed concentration upon an image that holds the psyche into a single place, that has a depressive effect. And therapy is concerned nowadays more and more with the frame, keeping the frame between the therapist and the patient, between the patient and his life, in keeping the vessel closed, keeping the *temenos* holy, keeping the analysis sealed—that is a Saturnian, melancholic method as well.

### The Picture of Depression

In getting hold of the symptoms of any psychological phenomenon, one does not necessarily use the patient's language as it is. The patient's language needs precision. When a patient goes to a physician and says, I have these pains in my stomach, the physician usually wants to know where in your stomach? Is it here? Or here? Does it spread? Is it sharp? He wants precision. If you have headaches, where do you have your headaches? Over the eyes? Pressure throughout your head? Again, he wants precision. We tend to forget the importance of precision in clinical work and that when a patient says, I have been feeling really depressed, we start from there. Maybe we should say, Tell me about it. Where do you feel depressed? When do you feel depressed? Oh, all the time. Do you feel depressed in the morning? What is it like when you get out of bed? Can you get out of bed? Get into the detail, the actual phenomenology of the condition. That seems to me, this step in the therapy, to be showing your interest in the condition rather than your interest in changing the condition, whatever the condition is. This is an act of love, being interested in what the person is, bringing in more detail. If your kid comes home and cries, I caught a fish! and you say, Great! That is not the same as saying, What kind of fish? Let me see it! How big is it? Where were you when you caught it? On the dock? What kind of bait did you use? That interest is a kind of love that is very different than praise, Great, you caught a fish! You are not interested, and it is the same way with the symptoms. It is that love of pathology or the love that comes into inquiry into pathology that I think makes a clinician. So, the person says that he is depressed—it may be that he is tired, or blue, or self-reflective. It may be crying, dryness, appetite, bowels, libido. It may be worry, guilt, sleep patterns, the diurnal rhythm. You want to ask about bowels, menstruation, libido, bathing and showering. Such a simple thing, but people who are seriously depressed stop bathing. And you know, the morning shower is one of the great antidepressants we have invented in America. I think that is the principle difference between the Europeans and the Americans. The Europeans take baths, and we shower. They sit and think, and we rush. You want to ask about eating habits and shopping. You want to get at the mood in general and also the thought content. What have you been thinking about? Because saying, I am depressed, does not really carry any weight. Nor do degrees of it, I am really depressed. I have been very depressed. You want much more than that. You want the phenomenology of it. The sense of it. The smell of it.

When are you depressed, where are you depressed, how are you depressed. Not why are you depressed. The why is a constant search for what is wrong, and it does not have images. It tries to explain, and that makes you feel worse because it will usually come up with blame: I am depressed because I treat my son so badly. I am depressed because I never made up with my father. I am depressed because..., because..., because..., for irredeemable reasons. But when are you depressed, how you are depressed, the images of the depression are what is important, and you can begin to imagine them rather than explain. Because one of the things that goes most dead is your imagination. It continues to repeat the same over and over.

And then, what goes on when you say you are depressed? Now usually the word is *nothing*—nothing goes on. Now I do not stop with that—I do not accept that as the answer. I think that is the first answer. I think there are things going on that one does not consider to be anything. You see what I am saying? The word *nothing* covers over what is going on. One thing that is going on is a feeling of emptiness or loss, or the quality of the nothing has its own quality of either grayness or blackness or emptiness or thickness—thickness is one of the words that is useful—a density, like having to move through a thickness—if you are moving, you move through a thickness so that is partly what slows everything down. By asking questions of this sort and observing in this way I am moving from a global way of looking at something to a particular way. I am making a therapeutic move, that is. I am drawing the patient's attention to particulars. Instead of "I am depressed" the patient's mind has to make the terrible effort of focusing on actual details of bowel movements, of sleep patterns. Attention is drawn to something, interest is asked for—my interest asks for interest. The adjectives—terrible, miserable, awful, dreadful, unbearable—describe pain, what the Swiss psychiatrist Eugen Bleuler—the father of Manfred—the one Jung worked with at the hospital in Zurich—said that "in general depression, all experiences, inner and outer, are toned with psychic pain of various kinds."[28] And that psychic pain is a psychiatrist's abstraction of words like terrible, miserable, awful, dreadful, unbearable—that everything feels that way—that is part of the psychic pain.

The expression in the face—remember I am talking about looking at the picture of depression—also the forehead is depressed. The forehead is a very important place in a person's body. You will notice that teenagers, unless they are doing the punk hair, generally, especially girls, cover their foreheads. All our politicians cover their foreheads now. All the TV announcers cover their foreheads. There is something strange about covering the forehead, I do not know what it is. The forehead once belonged to Hera, and the eyebrows belonged to Hera, and a woman who had a clear forehead was a woman of beauty. This was an important part of the face in portraiture. Covering the forehead, I do not know what that is about,

---

28. Eugen Bleuler, *Textbook of Psychiatry*, translated by A. A. Brill (New York: Macmillan, 1924), 119.

but I am suspicious of the TV people and politicians whose foreheads are not exposed. Teenagers are hiding out behind the bangs and the hair—that I understand—because that is part of staying sheltered in your hut until you are out of your hut. There is a ritual in that. The other seems a cover-up. But there is a depression in the forehead—lines that go this way—which is different than anxiety, which is narrowing and has fright in it, but the depressive forehead is much heavier and more horizontal. So there are lots of things to look at clinically—and I use the word clinically to mean being in the room with the patient. There are lots of things to look at so that you do not get caught by that word "depression," which is such a general word that you do not know what they are talking about. You do not know what they are talking about. Remember the language. The patient generally brings in collective language. When someone says, "phallic," that is a collective word, we do not know what it means any more. "Patriarchal" is another one. Also "journey," "creative"—these are words that are used now without any thought. They are slipshod—like using cheap money instead of real money. And so is the word "depression."

Instead of figuring it all out and having a large generalization about depression, when you are sitting with a person, the question is, "What is going on now?" Paying very close attention to the images, the feelings, the body parts, the thoughts that are actually present. It is, in a sense, an aesthetic activity, carefully working with whatever comes up, or whatever is there. It is a crafting or forming. Aristotle said the soul is the form of the body.[29] So as you are forming, you are soul-making. It is not enough to abreact, get it out of you, express it, because that is part of putting it behind you. "I had a good cry, and now I feel better." That is okay, too, but maybe the good cry wants more. If Emily Dickinson had good cries, I doubt we would have all that poetry. I think maybe she would have been happier. I do not know if happiness is the point. That is the great American problem, that happiness is supposed to be the point. It is absolutely declared, and we all subscribe to that. Other cultures would not subscribe to that. Crafting would be more important than turning the feeling to happiness.

---

29. *De Anima,* 412a20.

Now one thing that is important about depression is that it is, as they say, a disorder of mood, and it affects the entire personality. So it is also in your head, which feels heavy. In the contents of your head, in the weight of your legs. It is really an effort to get out of the chair. You can hear people who are more depressed, the sigh comes when they get up, there is a kind of weight to having to get yourself going. That belongs to the condition. It affects the whole personality and body. So the sense of being alone and isolated, uncared about by others, but also the lack of caring about yourself. That is why I mentioned the bathing. This is a nice description: "In general depression, all experiences are toned with psychic pain." And you can hear it in the voice. It tends to get monotone. The eyes get heavy. There is a kind of drooping of the eyelids. Nowadays there are so many older people who are depressed who have already had their lids lifted so you cannot see that, but that used to be one of the lovely indications of the depression, was this fold which dropped down. The limbs are often drawn in stiffly. The person looks older than they are, whereas the manic person usually looks younger, and their hair is glossy. The depressed person's hair is more like mine. Breathing is shallow and there are frequent sighs. Life is sort of flat and two-dimensional. And there is both a kind of torpidity on the one hand, and also there can be an active depression, a worried depression: Handwringing, pacing, nervousness. Usually, the forehead and the face show the depression with wrinkles, with downcast eyes, which is different—not necessarily anxious but pained. So you are reading a face. You are looking. You are picking up phenomena. It is extraordinary how this slowing down, this retraction of all psychic life affects such important things as breathing. The breathing becomes shallow and depressed people can more easily catch illnesses because of this retraction of the form of the body, the libido, the psychic energy. If you are not using your lungs, they are more susceptible to some illnesses—not being worked as they say.

So there are lots of tiny physical things that are important: constipation, insomnia, weight loss. Once I was in my physician's office getting whatever I needed done, and he was teaching that day some young intern. He kept insisting that she do some preliminary steps before this physical, and the one that she forgot was weighing the patient, putting the patient on the scale, because weight loss is one of the most important signs of depression.

Not all depression, because some people overeat and that is their mode of masking or carrying the depression, but weight loss is very important. And then you have to ask, "What time of day is it worse?" Is it worse in the morning, with the new day, as it often is? And the time of year. We think suicide is worse at Christmas, which is the most depressing time of the year, but, in fact, the curves of suicide peak in early summer.

There is a term they use from the Greek, *anhedonia*, meaning without any pleasure, that characterizes the entire life of a depressed person. I said earlier that everything is characterized by psychic pain, but everything is also characterized by the absence of pleasure, or as one writer put it, the absence of the mirth reflex. So you do not get very far joking.

It can come at any age—we mustn't think that depression belongs to old age or to a so-called mid-life crisis, this happy new invention of the bourgeoisie. Here's a poem from a nine year old girl:

All the flowers are drooping
And I am drooping too
Because I am sad and lonely
Like a bud almost in bloom.

The moments of sadness in childhood, the periods of depression in childhood, the times of feeling very lonely, very abandoned, very ugly, tired, unwanted, belong as much to childhood as they do to ages 35, 45, 85. It is a state of the soul.

So the question has to be, What does the soul want with these moods? Rather than thinking genetically, as if some kind of thing got kicked off in my chromosomes. What is the soul doing with these times of sadness? And, of course, there are very strong gender differences, but, traditionally, seventy-five percent of the people admitted to the hospital for depression are women. Traditionally, and that probably changes in different countries and different periods, but basically it seems to be a fact and, therefore, has a sociological implication that women in the last twenty years have begun to awaken to: that this is not necessarily a disease that I am carrying as a woman, but that this is a disease that belongs to the culture that women carry. People used to say that it always accompanied menopause, but it is all part of these fantasies about women that dominated psychiatry in the last century especially.

*Levels of Depression*

Let us try to remember those basic ideas: that the affective life in depression is sad, down, and low; that the activity or the will is inhibited, blocked, weakened; and that thoughts are few and narrow. Let us also try to remember that it is not a passing state. You see, there are levels of depression. This is a basic psychiatric question that comes up through the last couple centuries. What is the difference between feeling low because something unpleasant has happened—you have just been sick for a while and you have not fully recovered from the virus and feeling low and dumb and slow and depressed—and a full-blown psychotic depression where you believe your body parts are falling off, and your money is gone, and you have done everything possibly wrong with all your children and you are filled with hatred that is full of faces, colors, and monsters, and so on—psychotic delusions of depression. Now psychiatry has worked this problem for a long time. Is there an essential difference between the two, or is this merely a extreme quantity of depression? Is there a qualitative difference or only a quantitative difference? There are, so far, no valid means of measuring or figuring out if there is a qualitative difference or not. "There are no adequate quantitative and validated criteria for distinguishing pathological depression from normal mood swings or reactions to traumatic events." That is in an authoritative text book edited by Zubin and Freyhan.[30] So they tend to keep it on the same scale, and that we are all on different places on that scale at different times. At times when you have lost your job, or the bank has closed on you, or somebody has been promoted above you and you no longer have any future in the corporation, there is a reactive depression to that. Or when you have had to move to another city or are getting divorced, etc. And there are long periods of depression following that. A reactive depression is something that has happened in your so to speak "normal" life. You do not have delusions, you do not have fantasies that everything is falling apart, that you are dying or rotten in your gut and so on, but everything has slowed down. You are very low. That is a reactive depression. Now if that goes

---

30. Gerald L. Klerman, "Clinical Research in Depression," in *Disorders of Mood*, edited by Joseph Zubin and Fritz A. Freyhan (Baltimore and London: The Johns Hopkins Press, 1972), 174.

farther, and you do not come out of it, and you do not take any pills or have electroshock to get you out of it, then you will become delusional. You have paranoid delusions with a depressive tone. Some psychiatrists say there is a clear distinction between the ordinary, normal reactive response to a divorce and the psychotic.

I want to repeat that sentence again: "There are no adequate quantitative and validated criteria for distinguishing pathological depression from normal mood swings or reactions to traumatic events." In other words, when you are talking about feeling, there is no qualitative or validated criteria for distinguishing between psychotic and normal. I want to make that clear: what really qualifies a depression as pathological is delusion, not the intensity of the feeling. Now the virtue of that is that we can then begin to explore. We can move from it mainly being a mood disorder, or we can work with the mood in different ways instead of associating the mood as the cause or core of the depression. It may become clearer as we go along.

You see there are people who go through six or nine months—nine months being the more statistically correct for the length for the cyclical depressive part—of very serious stagnation, stuck in this mood. The soul may be going through something very important, even if it is full of psychic pain. But I would not call the person sick in the pathological sense, in the way psychiatry would use the term. You may want to medicate in order to relieve the pain, but that is a different thing. Part of the sickness is how much you can take—it is subjective.

I think, anytime there is a major change, there is a major loss. We all want change, but nobody wants the shadow side of change that is losing what came before. So every time you gain, you lose. We have separated the winners from the losers in the culture to such an extent that we forget that every time we praise a winner such as a lottery winner who is one in ten million, we have 9,999,999 losers. Or every time we have a foot race or an ice-skating event, we have one winner and ten losers. Our emphasis on winning in America creates a nation of losers.

So we have had what you would call normal reactions to what we would call tragic events or simply losses. Time has to be given to that. And depression forces you to give time to that. You follow me there? If there is a divorce or death, the depressed condition that you feel forces you to give time to that event. You do not get over it that quickly. There is also another type of response that is more of a neurotic reaction. There is a disproportion between the stimulus and the response. Your dog got hit and run over, and you are knocked out for a year. Now I do not know how long you are supposed to mourn for a dog—I am not setting up a standard that two weeks is good enough to do it. But it may be that a ritual is called for that has not been performed, or that the dog represents a great deal more, or that the dog's death coincides with changes in your own life that you have not noticed, and that there is a loss of a much larger extent that is going on, or that the dog symbolizes all the losses, all the tragedies, and all the absences of love. But there are these reactions, what used to be called "neurotic reactions," that are exaggerated, or prolonged, or do not quite fit the pattern of working through grief or loss or mourning. They can be autochthonous—coming out of nowhere—you just begin to feel depressed. You had a flu, and after the flu, you continued to be exhausted, and for six or eight months you felt depressed. You could not get back into your life. It is as if it happens for its own sake. These are the interesting ones, for they are not really tied to an external cause.

There is a kind of depression that is on the official lists or categorized that I want to introduce now. I do not know if it is neurotic or not, but certain people who have melancholic temperaments more than the other sorts of temperaments or who are engaged in certain kinds of lonely occu-pations—writers are notorious for this—tend to have more depressions in their lives. Also I think ethnic background and geography are involved in this: where you live, the seasons of the year, the ethnic patterns of your people. And then it becomes really a cross-cultural question of how different peoples live the depressive moments of their lives. What is the difference between the Berbers of North Africa who live in vast expanses and the fishing communities of northern Norway? What are the different ways they live the melancholy of their geographies? People in the North versus those in the South. There is a longstanding, I think almost archetypal belief, at least in the northern hemisphere, that northern peoples are of a certain sort, and southern peoples are of another sort. I have read an anthropological report that people who live on the north side of Iceland regard the people who live on the south side of Iceland as sluggish, lazy, hanging out, not working, dedicated to fun. The words used for the peoples living on the south shores of Iceland are very similar to used by the northern Italians for the Sicilians.

When I learned psychopathology in Switzerland, we were taught, in making a diagnosis, to be sure you are talking to a Swiss person and to find out from which part of Switzerland they come from, because the behavior of Bavarians is so manic that if you do not realize a person is from Bavaria, you will call this person manic. Whereas if that kind of behavior were observed about a Swiss from the inner cantons of Switzerland, they would really be psychotic, because that is not the way anybody who lives there in those granite rocky villages would behave. So the geography and the region and the way people are is very important.

### Differentiating Depression from Melancholy

There is a connection between melancholy and beauty. There is a theory of beauty that appears in Thomas Aquinas and reappears in James Joyce's *Portrait of an Artist as a Young Man* where Stephen Dedalus introduces his theory of aesthetics.[31] This theory of beauty defines what beauty does and how you recognize beauty. *Beauty arrests motion.* It stops you. Now that is on the personal level, but the point is that it gives you the stasis that is the eternal, so there is a relation between beauty and the ideal. It is a whole theory of art. But the notion that beauty arrests motion makes it clearer that arresting motion might give you beauty. So it makes it a little clearer why melancholy or depression or sadness or slowing down gives you more of a chance of your being open to beauty. It does not mean that a racing gazelle across the plain is not a beautiful image—but you are stopped when you see it—Ah!—or that moments of beauty are not fleeting or ephemeral, but, again, it is something that stops you.

My theme has been that depression is the secular form of melancholy. It is melancholy without the gods, so you are simply left with depression. If we have, in the manic state, an elation of feeling, a hyper-activity of

---

31. On Joyce and Aquinas, see Frederick K. Lang, *Ulysses and the Irish God* (Lewisburg: Bucknell University Press; London and Toronto: Associated University Presses, 1983), 45ff.

willing, and a flight of ideas, in depression it is just the reverse. The thoughts are few and narrow, the emotion is sad and low, and activity is severely inhibited. In fact, the first sign of a clinical depression—"clinical" referring to somebody who we think should be treated—is that they cannot move. In Switzerland, a person says, *Ich habe es nicht geschafft* (I could not do it). Now that is a big thing. Switzerland still operates with the work ethic—despite the value of their money—and not being able to do the work, not being able to get up and go to work is a critical indication. It is about the inhibition of will, that is, the entire lowering of all thought and activity. But particularly I am emphasizing the will here, the ability to move, to do things, the enormous effort it takes during the depressed phase to do anything, to get dressed even.

Now one thing we need to realize is that all the things we say are time-bound. That is, not just time-bound by the clock, but time-bound by history. The notions that we have of sadness, and what is going on inside the brain all belong to our time. The idea of depression, and the whole notion that there are mood disorders, was introduced by John Haslam, another one of these psychiatrists who lived with his patients in England, in 1798.[32] Now, Wordsworth and Coleridge's lyrical ballads also entered the world in 1798, and it is the date when everyone says the Romantic movement officially began. So John Haslam's text, which classified mania and melancholy, and which began to use the term "disorders of mood," enters our way of thinking at that same time. He wanted to define insanity in terms of mood rather than in terms of intellectual disorders: disorders of thinking, illogical thinking, concretistic thinking, other kinds of disorders of thinking. All through our Western culture at the time, there was this emphasis on a shift from the importance of thinking to the importance of feeling, following Rousseau and the German Romantics. In other words, it was the culmination of the eighteenth century's working on the feeling faculty that elevated the realm of sadness and depression into an important kind of disorder. And it was important because there was a cultural interest in what was going on in the realm of feeling.

---

32. John Haslam, *Observations on Insanity: With Practical Remarks on the Disease, and an Account of the Morbid Appearances on Dissection* (London: F. and C. Rivington, 1798).

Another part of the history of our field is this: in the next century, a hundred years later, it began to move away from classifying disorders into typologies and structures and endless numbers of what they called taxonomies or nosologies, to what the Germans called a *Krankheitsbild*—an *image* of the illness. They began to work from the presentation of the illness, what it looks like, not what is going on behind the scenes. You did not work from the concept of the depression, you worked from the phenomenology of what you saw. The DSM was the last phase of that. You get descriptions of what the behavior is, of what you *see.* Unfortunately, a new move has begun, away from the image of the illness back to the explanation of the illness. We are going backwards, so that when you ask about a person, it begins with a story about their mother or their childhood abuse—something to do with an explanation rather than a phenomenological depiction.

I was at a party one night and talking to a man about somebody else's divorce—this was a man who ran a liquor shop and who was not involved with psychology in any way—and I asked him something about what was going on, and he began to describe the sister-in-law in terms of what happened to her in childhood, what the father was like. He began to do a radio-TV analysis rather than telling me that these people were fighting all day long, or that he had hit her, or that she was spending money like crazy. There was no description! There is all this second-level psychologizing. Now the great move that German psychiatry made at the end of the last century was to return to the description of the phenomena—what is the *Bild,* the image? What are you seeing there in front of you? What are you looking at? And how does it present itself? And never mind the underlying causes, the case history. The case history is a fiction. It is a form of fiction writing. It is a form of story telling. For that argument, for that whole discussion of the fiction of case history, you might read my book *Healing Fiction,*[33] about how fiction writing captures us into belief in stories, and how we go to therapists to get our stories edited and maybe even rewritten to get a better story. Because you really do take your biography enormously literally. This is the literalization of your biography. You are

---

33. James Hillman, *Healing Fiction* (Thompson: Conn.: Spring Publications, 2019 [1983]).

so identified with that biography, because therapy has identified you with your biography rather than with your description. If you read good novels, you do not really get a lot of explanation of why a person is as he is, you get a description of how he behaves. If you go to the theater, it is all about the actions, says Aristotle—how they reveal character. How they do what they do—their gestures, their language, their pauses, their connections—and you do not know if this woman on the stage did such-and-such when she was thirty-two, or that when she was twelve something happened, and so on. That is not part of it. It is what is happening in the act, during the scene. And if you take it very strictly, what is not present simply *is not.* That is another sense of fiction. But we are very hung up on the story that precedes the presentation. One of the great virtues of medicine has always been a careful observation of the patient, and that is one of the reasons physicians so often disregard the patient's story. Of course, they want to hear the medical history, but not the patient's interpretation of it. They want to keep their mind open for observation.

The main complaint that people have during clinical admission is, I can't cope and I can't go on. It is very similar to what I said about the Swiss who said, I can't get up to work. You can see the sense of how much this enormously manic culture demands of one. Coping. Most of us do not have enough time. How to make time? We want to make time, find time, and the pressure to be on time and to meet deadlines. So saying that I cannot cope and I cannot go on means that I cannot live this manic life. That is what is being said here. Now, of course, there are also organic and senile depressions, where depression is an accompaniment of physical changes. And some of it has to be considered to be separation depression—that is, when the significant other, like the mother of a small child dies, where the anaclitic, the leaning on the other, the dependency, creates a strong depressive condition. And I do wonder whether in chemical dependency, the withdrawal from that on which you are leaning leaves you not only with withdrawal symptoms but also with depression. So depression becomes a crucial issue in endless areas of our life, not only our clinical life but in all aspects of our life.

There is an obsessive quality that belongs to depression. The thoughts return to the same obsessive ruminations. Particularly the sense of being inadequate: I really fucked up my life. The sense that one should never have gotten divorced, or left that job, or moved to California... That kind of obsessive sense of having ruined one's life belongs to depression. Now, of course, these thoughts occur in all our lives. But it is the obsessiveness of it, the domination of the idea. The mind is constantly ruminating. Even if one is not wringing one's hands and pacing the floor, the mind is. The mind is ruminating about guilt and failure and inadequacy. It does not look back with pleasure. And there are destructive fantasies of every sort, about one's body, about money, the haunted sense that you are going to be impoverished. The bag-lady fantasy, and the sense that everything is getting worse, a sense of doom. I had a Swiss patient once who used to come in regularly and say, *Es wird immer schlimmer* (It is getting worse and worse)—remorse, a sense of failure. And forgiveness does not work, which is part of the suicide problem. The kind of remorse where you feel that the only way out is to leave the world, because you will only do more wrong by being here. So these are partially delusional ideas determined by mood.

There is also a lack of energy and an inability to concentrate, to pay attention, or make decisions. This is one of the things that bothers people terribly during a depression. They cannot make a decision. Being required to make a decision can even instigate a depression. If you follow Jung and look at everything that is going on in the psyche with a purposive eye—even if we do not know what the purpose is—then we might look at it to see what would be the purpose of not being able to concentrate? Not being able to pay attention? Not being able to decide? It is clear that one thing happening is that the old ego is nonfunctional. And the depression has robbed the old ego of its main activities: attention, concentration, decision. Maybe the mind needs to focus on other things. Now this produces lots of trouble because you are caught in adding to the hatred of yourself. Not only are you worried that you are inadequate, not only did you fuck up your life when you look back, you are now fucking it up again! Right now I can't decide. Right now I can't even re-do. I don't know what to do.

The waiting, the longing, is for that to lift. When it is severe, the waiting is not a waiting for things to turn up better. It is a Beckett-like waiting room. It is *Waiting for Godot*. It is simply waiting, without any expectation of anything. You cannot even imagine a future except blackly. Things will get worse, they are getting worse, the end of the line is disease, death, and doom. You are not waiting for redemption. That is why these ideas that there is light at the end of the tunnel, that Easter follows good Friday—that is all a waste of time. That does not touch the sense of nothingness—that "nothingness" is the main feeling. You are sitting in nothingness, and that can be a waiting, but there is no hope.

I have already pointed out the lack of energy, the psycho-motor constriction, the slowing down and the heavy legs. There is a disappearance of sex, appetite, sleep; there is constipation, weight loss, and so on. In the old psychiatry, this used to be a condition associated with maturity and late life. But it no longer is. Adolescence may be very depressed, and you may remember depression as part of your own adolescence, and even childhood. It appears a little differently in younger people, as cynicism and bitterness and a kind of social hatred as well as self-hatred. And it is difficult for a fifteen-year-old to have a place for this. And as you know, in the US today, childhood adolescent suicides are increasing.

I want to emphasize again these basic criteria that I tried to describe in my own language with more detail than what one gets in the general descriptions of mood disorders. I mean, "markedly diminished interest or pleasure" is a pretty weak way of describing the despair that comes with depression. To call it diminished interest or pleasure—we all have diminished interest or pleasure in all kinds of things regularly. That does not give you the feeling of that retardation or tell where it is—it is in the legs, it is in the head, and it is the sense that the body is far too heavy to lift up and move somewhere so everything is slowed down. Feelings of worthlessness. Recurrent thoughts of death.

Robert Burton wrote three volumes on melancholy, and this is what he says in 1621: "It is a disease so grievous, so common, I know not wherein to do a more general service, and spend my time better, than to prescribe means how to prevent and cure so universal a malady, an epidemical disease, that so often, so much, crucifies the body and mind."[34] He uses the word "crucifies" here, which leads us to modes of thinking about how

---

34. Robert Burton, *The Anatomy of Melancholy*, 3 vols. (London: George Bell and Sons, 1896), 1: 138.

to move the depression. If it is imagined against the background of the crucifixion and the dark night of the soul, then there is an imagination of resurrection and recovery. But when a person is in that condition, nailed to the cross, there is no use talking about the day the tomb will be opened and you will be risen again. In fact, it is insulting, because you are not talking to the patient, you are talking to your own wish. There is no image of relief. That is why in alchemy they used the metal lead for Saturn and the depressive condition because lead is the heaviest of the metals. It is the one metal that X-rays will not go through. You cannot see through depression. When you are in it, you do not have images, you cannot see through into its causes, into what is going on, you are only caught by it.

There are certain qualities of depression that seem to be contemporary, that are different from the classical descriptions, especially in younger people and in children. Some of these terms do not fit in the old way—the hostility, the closed-off-ness, the exaggerated self-pity. I do not know what comes first. Does this come first and does depression emerge from this? Or are these side-components of the depression? I do not know. And there are the disturbed life patterns that are, in a sense, disturbed cultural patterns—the disturbances of eating habits, drug use, family life, and moving from place to place. But one quality of it that seems genuinely to belong to the pictures of depression in young people and today's children, is the occurrence of radical mood swings. The mood swings are shorter in duration and more radical. And exaggerated self-pity, and also hostility. But you see hostility all through adolescence. It is appropriate. Sullen. Isolated. Different. I am not so sure that this belongs to depression. I can see many of these qualities belonging to the realm of initiations—the requirement for initiations—the not-yet being in your peer group, not having found your peer group, not having found the relationships that you belong in. This is why gangs are so important—for offering that. There is so much present in an adolescent, all the seeds are there, so all the syndromes are there. We would have to single out the depressive element and see what really belongs to depression there. And that also includes the suicides of adolescents and children because all suicide does not belong to depression—suicide belongs to all kinds of other things as well.

There is a depressive moment running through all adolescence. Think of your own adolescence. Think of your years between twelve and twenty. Think of the crying that you did, the loneliness that you felt, the self-pity that you endured and enjoyed, the long lugubrious sadnesses, the exile you felt, the thoughts of death, god, and mystery. I mean all the things that go on in that period! You realize that depression is part of that phase of life in our world. There is a depressive streak. It is also the extreme sensitivity to beauty and to loss. With anorexia, the patterns of life are not necessarily immobilized and depressed. Very often anorexic girls are very active, to keep their weight down. They are swimming all day long, they are working out, they are cooking for friends, there is a lot of activity, and you cannot believe that someone who looks like that and has so little substance is so active. Now we could call it a mass depression, but that does not mean a thing. I am not so sure that we should put anorexia and bulimia in the bed of depression. They may belong to another group of disturbances.

Inherent in the idea of depression is also that it is trying to get us to shut down for one reason or another. Being on the inside of a depression, the body can shut down, but the mind is more active than ever. It is a manic way to stay out of the dark hole. So it is a fallacy that someone can go lay on a beach and heal, because when you are in a depressed state, time is a son of a bitch. I mean, it is the last thing you want, and it is a painful way to be, so in spite of the idea that outwardly we are shutting down, inwardly it is quite the opposite. And it is more active than ever, and that is what I think makes recovery so difficult. The inward activity is very, very important. When we come to discuss Saturn and the myths, we will see that the inward activity belongs to the archetype, which sometimes manifests outwardly in what once was called agitated depression, pacing back and forth all night long, handwringing, worrying, insomnia, so that the mental activity, the fury, actually enters somatically.

*Hope & Beauty*

We are also going to have to talk about hope and hopelessness. Is it hopelessness or is it apathy? Remember that the doors to the underworld said: "All hope abandon ye who enter here."[35] I think it is very difficult to

---

35. Dante Alighieri, *Inferno*, 3.9 (trans. H.F. Cary).

understand the absence of hope unless one knows something, as a clinician, about the underworld. That is what I meant by clinical education. You can learn a great deal about what to do technically and what the drugs are and the dosages and the laws and the DSM, but if you do not know the culture that the language of depression is speaking about and to, you have nothing to meet the patient with, as a clinician.

I am struggling with whether I want to get into this question of hope. You see, I am hopeless myself, and I am accused of hopelessness. I have abandoned the idea of hope completely. I do not see it as a virtue. I think it takes us completely out of the present and sets up fantasies that do not happen and leads to despair, and I think that if you give up hope, you also give up despair. No hope, no despair. You are out of that whole game. And the emphasis on hope as a virtue is an extraordinary trap to keep everybody manic and pushing forward. Now I am sure this will meet with opposition from Christians and forward-looking people. But I think we need to think very carefully about the acceptance of hope uncritically.

The great question is, and Michael Ventura and I talked about this in our book,[36] how do you live when the ship is going down? How do you live if you have abandoned hope? Now, the Greek idea was very different because they had Elpis ($\dot{\epsilon}\lambda\pi\acute{\iota}s$), the spirit of hope, who was the last item in Pandora's box or jar. Pandora's curiosity opened the lid, and as all the spites flew out into the world, she slammed down the lid just in time to keep hope inside. All the evils are out in the world, but hope is inside. And it keeps pushing us. It is "the force that through the green fuse drives the flower."[37] It is that constant green hope that will lead us, start us up again, get us going and so on. But must you have hope in order to get going? That is a question. Must you hope? Saint Paul warns against the hopes that we conjure with.[38] T. S. Elliot refers to that warning in Saint Paul and puts it in the Four Quartets: "I said to my soul, be still, and wait without

---

36. James Hillman and Michael Ventura, We've Had a Hundred Years of Psychotherapy —and the World's Getting Worse (San Francisco: HarperSanFrancisco, 1992).

37. The Poems of Dylan Thomas, edited by Daniel Jones (New York, New Directions, 1952), 77.

38. "For in hope we were saved. Now hope that sees for itself is not hope. For who hopes for what one sees? But if we hope for what we do not see, we wait with endurance" (Romans 8:24–25).

hope/For hope would be hope for the wrong thing."[39] So I think that one of the events that goes on in depression is giving up hope. Living without hope. That is a whole other way of living. Hope always has future time in it. I will get better, it will go away. I have a little sign that somebody gave me at one of these seminars. It says, "Owing to the energy crisis, the light at the end of the tunnel has been turned off!" So, how do you keep moving, living, thinking, feeling, and all the other things there are in the world, without hope? You can even plan, I think, but I wonder about the need for hope.

Let me read to you from William Styron's memoir, *Darkness Visible*:

> A phenomenon that a number of people have noted while in deep depression is the sense of being accompanied by a second self—a wraith-like observer, who, not sharing the dementia of his double, is able to watch with dispassionate curiosity as his companion struggles against the oncoming disaster or decides to embrace it. There is a theatrical quality about all this, and during the next several days as I went about stolidly preparing for extinction [he was preparing for his suicide], I could not shake off a sense of melodrama—a melodrama in which I, the victim-to-be of self-murder, was both the solitary actor and lone member of the audience [so something was accompanying him]. I had not as yet chosen the mode of my departure... [40]

That is a very interesting phenomenon. There is a book by Mary Watkins called *Invisible Guests*[41] that deals with these figures you speak with and that come to you, that are manifestations perhaps of the invisibles or of your particular *daimon*. Now, I do want to say one thing also, since I have opened Styron's book. You do not have to move through depression, or you do not have to get out of the black in order to get into the white in the alchemical process. In other words, you do not have to see it as a stage, because by seeing it as a stage, as I have been trying to say all along, you

---

39. "East Coker," in T.S. Eliot, *Four Quartets* (New York: Harcourt, Brace and Company, 1943), 15.

40. William Styron, *Darkness Visible: A Memoir of Madness* (New York: Random House, 1990).

41. Mary Watkins, *Invisible Guests: The Development of Imaginal Dialogues* (Hillsdale, N.J.: The Analytic Press, 1986).

have it as part of a Good Friday to Easter Sunday fantasy. But it is not a stage. The *nigredo* is not a stage. These are *states* of the soul, each having its own substantive, essential value. Nonetheless, in some times and in some people and in some cases, there is a movement from black to blue, or a movement of one sort or another. I want to read another excerpt from Styron's book. He is a very good novelist (he wrote *Sophie's Choice*, as you may know):

> My wife had gone to bed, and I had forced myself to watch the tape of a movie in which a young actress, who had been in a play of mine, was cast in this small part. At one point in the film, which was set in late-nineteenth-century Boston, the characters moved down the hallway of a music conservatory, beyond the walls of which, from unseen musicians, came a contralto voice, a sudden soaring passage from the Brahms *Alto Rhapsody*.
>
> This sound, which like all music—indeed, like all pleasure—I had been numbly unresponsive to for months, pierced my heart like a dagger, and in a flood of swift recollection I thought of all the joys the house had known: the children who had rushed through its rooms, the festivals, the love and work, the honestly earned slumber, the voices and the nimble commotion, the perennial tribe of cats and dogs and birds...All this I realized was more than I could ever abandon [when he was on the edge of the suicide], even as what I had set out so deliberately to do was more than I could inflict on those memories, and upon those, so close to me, with whom those memories were bound. And just as powerfully I realized I could not commit this desecration on myself. I drew upon some last gleam of sanity to perceive the terrifying dimensions of the mortal predicament I had fallen into. I woke up my wife and soon telephone calls were made, and the next day I was admitted to the hospital.[42]

So instead of killing himself, he went to hospital. But what is really striking is the moment of Brahms's *Alto Rhapsody*. The contralto voice. We sometimes forget the tremendous, overwhelming power of beauty and the soul's desperate hunger for beauty.

Even in those who are destroyed by what is called desperate clinical depression, you see that there is a beauty in their faces, especially in the

---

42. Styron, *Darkness Visible*, 66–67.

eyes. There is some extraordinary mystery there that people who are engaged in therapy must respect—that mystery that goes on in the work, that is going on in the soul of people in these agonies.

In Styron's case, the timeliness is extremely important. That is, the timeliness in the sense that he was right, he had gone to the farthest intense place of his decision about suicide. So the timeliness—I would not call it synchronicity—but the timeliness of the exaggeration, of going as far as possible, perhaps then made it possible for something else to happen. Jung might call it *enantiodromia*, the turning into the opposite. As he was closest to suicide, there came the sudden realization of the beauty of life. I think one important thing here is that the slash into the heart for him was not love from wife, children or therapist. It was this piercing pain of beauty that opened him up to the memories of children. It was not relationship! It was not transference. It was none of the therapeutic moves, the empathy, the relationships and so on. It was beauty. Exquisite, high-culture beauty. Doesn't have to be high culture beauty, but it has to be beauty. In his case it was high-culture beauty.

It happened at a certain critical moment, when the thing had gone to the very extreme. Things do not turn sometimes until they go to the extreme, and that is so difficult therapeutically. I wrote *Suicide and the Soul*[43] to approach that particular question, How do you know? What is suicide intervention doing? We do not know what the soul wants by going to the death experience. We do not know. And I do not mean that you are supposed to kill yourself. You see what I am saying? What does the soul want in going to the end, into that intensity? That it is so difficult for the therapist to accompany these conditions was why I wrote that book in 1964, which is a long time ago. I began to work on it in 1962, so I must have realized that this is the whole initiation into being a therapist. Can you "walk with" somebody into the bottom? Unless I have some perspective on this—Camus said, suicide is "the only truly serious philosophical problem. Judging whether life is or is not worth living amounts to answering the fundamental question of philosophy."[44] Why does anybody want to live

---

43. James Hillman, *Suicide and the Soul* (Thompson, Conn.: Spring Publications, 2020 [1964].

44. Albert Camus, *The Myth of Sisyphus and Other Essays*, translated by Justin O'Brien (New York: Vintage Books, 1955), 3.

at all? And no matter how you are trained, you have to have a cosmology into which these things fit. You have to develop some kind of philosophy about it. And it is interesting that all that wonderful life that flooded back, flooded back only when Styron was struck to the heart by this voice.

Styron's book is an excellent report for many reasons. It is very well written, but another reason is that he speaks so well of the psychiatric clinic, and that is something. Therapists that do not come from the medical background usually hate the clinic. They have this built-in prejudice against the clinic, whereas the clinic offers a container, a peace, a regularity, the end of responsibility and the burden of life. We do not have to think of the clinic as the place where you get drugged and zapped, but as a refuge. And that is worth thinking about before you go off the deep end about how terrible the medical model is!

*More Differentiation*

One of the major thinkers of the Renaissance was Marcilio Ficino. There is a book of his, which Charles Boer translated, called *The Book of Life*.[45] Ficino claims that he was a child of Saturn, that is, that he was a melancholic man his whole life, a miserable melancholic. He was partly hunchbacked. He was a Dominican priest, which is a depressing thing in itself. He was an extraordinary translator of Greek works into Latin and Italian. He was always thinking, I am a melancholic, I am depressed, how can I sing the right songs, make the right music to the planets, so that I can move out of being a child only to Saturn and into Venus, which would make life sweeter, nicer, easier? And he comes up with recommendations. He says you cannot move directly from Saturn to Venus. That would be like a conversion. That would be like bringing a young virgin to the old King David—if you remember, that goes on in the Bible.[46] You cannot just make that move from one to the other. He said you have to pass first through Jupiter or the Sun. There is a kind of progression. But whenever one is

45. Marsilio Ficino, *The Book of Life*, translated by Charles Boer (Thompson, Conn.: Spring Publications, 2024 [1980]).

46. 1 Kings 1–4: "When King David was very old, he could not keep warm even when they put covers over him. So his attendants said to him, "Let us look for a young virgin to serve the king and take care of him. She can lie beside him so that our lord the king may keep warm."

depressed, one question always comes up: How can I get out of this? But you do not get out; you make room for others to move in. You move it from depression to melancholy. You expand the depression through imagination, through arts, and so on. You feed the god in the depression with material, not with introspection.

Let me read you a few descriptions to see if you think these people are talking about depression or not. This is Gerald Manley Hopkins:

> How to keep—is there any any, is there none such, nowhere
>     known some, bow or brooch or braid or brace, lace, latch
>     or catch or key to keep
> Back beauty, keep it, beauty, beauty, beauty,...from vanish-
>     ing away?
> O is there no frowning of these wrinkles, ranked wrinkles
>     deep,
> Down? no waving off of these most mournful messengers,
>     still messengers, sad and stealing messengers of grey?
> No there's none, there's none, O no there's none,
> Nor can you long be, what you now are, called fair,
> Do what you may do, what, do what you may,
> And wisdom is early to despair:
> Be beginning; since, no, nothing can be done
> To keep at bay
> Age and age's evils, hoar hair,
> Ruck and wrinkle, drooping, dying, death's worst, winding
>     sheets, tombs and worms and tumbling to decay;
> So be beginning, be beginning to despair.
> O there's none; no no no there is none:
> Be beginning to despair, to despair,
> Despair, despair, despair, despair.[47]

Does that poem sound like depression to you? It is called the "Leaden Echo." How about this one:

> I have of late—but wherefore I know not—lost all my mirth, fore-
> gone all custom of exercise; and indeed it goes so heavily with

47. "The Leaden Echo and the Golden Echo," in *Poems of Gerard Manley Hopkins,* edited by Robert Bridges (New York and London: Oxford University Press, 1948), 96–97.

> my disposition that this goodly frame, the earth, seems to me a
> sterile promontory. This most excellent canopy, the air, look you,
> this brave o'erhanging firmament, this majestical roof fretted
> with golden fire—why, it appears no other thing to me than a foul
> and pestilent congregation of vapours. What a piece of work is
> man! How noble in reason, how infinite in faculties! in form and
> moving, how express and admirable, in action how like an angel,
> in apprehension, how like a god—the beauty of the world, the
> paragon of animals! And yet, to me, what is this quintessence of
> dust? Man delights not me—no, nor woman neither...

You probably know that one. It is from *Hamlet*.[48] Hamlet, the melancholic
Dane. Is he depressed? Is he delusional? Is that the speech of depression?
What is in the passage? He is perceiving the overhanging firmament. He is
not using depressed language. It is very energized. Hopkins says "despair"
six times He says "no" three times. King Lear says "never" five times.[49]
"Never, never, never, never, never"—that repetition, that same few thoughts,
that narrowness. There is just stasis. That is depressive language.

St. Thomas writes about a sin that in the Middle Ages was called
*acedia* (sloth)—which was a dryness of the spirit that is comparable to
what we call depression or what people have equated with depression:
"Acedia does not move to action, but strongly hinders action."[50] Thomas
was extraordinary in his ability to summarize everything into marvelous
phrases. The problem of inaction in Hamlet could be understood from
this point of view as his having suffered from depression because action
requires the ability of the will to perform, and there is an inhibition of
the will.

Hamlet says "lost all my mirth." He has had it all already—well he has
not had Ophelia...as far as we know...that is still obscure...The point
here is there is beauty in his speech, which *could* make it melancholy, but
there is also a curious self-division. It is much more schizophrenic in the
sense that he is feeling one way, but his language goes another way. His
language is rich, expansive, full of extraordinary phrases: "this majestical
roof fretted with golden fire—why, it appears no other thing to me but a

---

48. *The Tragedy of Hamlet, Prince of Denmark,* Act 2, Scene 2.
49. *King Lear,* Act 5, Scene 3.
50. *Summa Theologiae,* II-II, Q. 35.

foul and pestilent congregation of vapours." That is what he is saying, but can you feel that split in there? That disassociation between perceptions and feelings? Things are going on different tracks at the same time. He is much more interesting. Let me follow that with a passage from Keats that you probably know very well too. This is the third stanza of the *Ode to a Nightingale*:

> Fade far away, dissolve, and quite forget
>> What thou among the leaves hast never known,
> The weariness, the fever, and the fret
>> Here, where men sit and hear each other groan;
> Where palsy shakes a few, sad, last gray hairs,
>> Where youth grows pale, and spectre-thin, and dies;
>>> Where but to think is to be full of sorrow
>>> And leaden-eyed despairs;
>>> Where Beauty cannot keep her lustrous eyes,
>> Or new Love pine at them beyond to-morrow.[51]

Here, the language is much more cohesive with the mood, and this is, to my mind, much more melancholic because the beauty of the language, the beauty of the emotions and the despair are all interwoven. In that passage from Hamlet, they are not.

> Darkling I listen; and, for many a time
>> I have been half in love with easeful Death,
> Call'd him soft names in many a mused rhyme,
>> To take into the air my quiet breath;
> Now more than ever seems it rich to die,
>> To cease upon the midnight with no pain.[52]

That is another passage from Keats's *Ode to a Nightingale*.

Have you ever dissolved in tears? The experience of dissolution, falling apart? A suicidal reflection is in the second half of the poem: "Darkling I listen and for many a time / I have been half in love with easeful Death, / ... Now more than ever it seems it rich to die / To cease upon the midnight with no pain." This is his suicidal moment.

---

51. *Complete Poems and Selected Letters of John Keats* (New York: The Modern Library, 2001), 236.

52. Ibid., 237.

One of the problems here is that we are talking about people who were geniuses in their extraordinary ability to express these things. The desire to dissolve, to let go, to let it all dissolve and drop out, the kind of suicide that involves pills or the gas or the auto exhaust—not the stabbing or the hanging. The *kind* of suicide is very important—this is easefulness, peacefulness. I think that is a dark moment of depression there.

Now let me read you one more. This is a passage from Denis Diderot who wrote this on 31 October 1760 to his friend Sophie Volland. He asked a mutual friend, a Scotsman by the name of Hoop, to describe was then called the "spleen"or the "English vapors." Spleen meant hypochondria, neurosis, a kind of depressive condition when you cannot get it together, or as we would say, can't get your shit together. That would be the English spleen. Diderot quotes this passage, so in a sense it is both in Hoop's language and Diderot's version of the language:

> For twenty years now I have been subject to a general malaise of a more or less annoying nature; my head is never free. Sometimes it is as heavy that it is like a weight pulling you forward, which might precipitate you from a window into the street, or to the bottom of a river if you were standing at its edge. My ideas are somber, and I'm consumed by sorrow and ennui... Do you know that sort of stupor or ill humor on awakening after having slept too long? That is my usual state. I'm disgusted with life; the slightest variations of the weather are like violent jolts for me; I wouldn't know how to stay in one place. I have to leave without knowing where I'm going. It's like I did the tour of the world... I'm completely out of tune with others. I dislike what they like, I like what they dislike; there are days when I hate light, and others when it reassures me. My nights are agitated by a thousand bizarre dreams...I have never known such despair. I'm old, decrepit, impotent...But...the most troublesome sensation is to be aware of one's own stupidity.[53]

Now for an intellectual, this is a tough one. With all your training and your good mind, and all the rest of it you cannot figure out why you are so miserable. You are utterly stupid vis-à-vis a depression. Also he speaks

---

53. Quoted in Reinhard Kuhn, *The Demon of Noontide: Ennui in Western Literature* (Princeton, N.J.: Princeton University Press, 1976), 163.

about his head pulling him forward. What is the phrase he uses? "My head is never free."

One of the kinds of eighteenth- and nineteenth-century genre painting, and then all the way up through Matisse and Picasso, is an image of the *anima*, a portrait of a woman holding her head, maybe asleep, a bit of sewing on her lap, a book open, sitting in front of a mirror holding her head. This is a classic position, going all the way back to the Renaissance, and probably earlier: your hand holding your head up. This immense heaviness of the head. What is all that about? What is this head that has become so heavy? Probably you know this feeling. It is not just having a headache; it is so heavy that you cannot hold your head up, except with your hand. This is one of the depressive postures. Your hand is the extension of yourself into the world, with your arms going out into the world: the reacher, the consumer, the shopper, the doer, the handler, the manipulator. The Greek word for this is *orexsis* (ὄρεξις), appetite, desire, from which we have *anorexia*. Appetite is indicated by the extension of the hand into the world. So that is stopped. The depression has brought that hand in. It can only hold up your head. It has left the world. Your head has sucked your hand out of the world. Maybe your hand is metaphorically sorting out your head. Maybe that is what is going on. Your hand has been drawn to your head in order to work through, figure out, sort through, separate, distinguish, discriminate, all this stuff in the head. So something is going on, but it is going on in your head. And in that sense, we can go back to Hamlet and imagine that all those words that are whirling about the world as part of what is going on in his head. Our heads can be very occupied in depression. Even if it is the same thought again and again. In other words, it can be an agitation in the head, not just the hand-wringing depression, pacing the room, but that the head is gripped by something. And, as you know, thought is very, very hard work, and that is one reason I think we do not do it very much. And so you really do need a hand.

One of the cautions that are given in psychiatry or abnormal psychology or psychotherapy is that you do not do psychotherapy with depressives. Because you only drive the person deeper into their recriminations, their miseries, their blames, their finding fault with themselves. You only make

Louis Jean-François Lagrenée
*La Mélancolie,* c. 1785
Oil on canvas
Musée du Louvre, Paris

it worse. That is what they are already doing, making themselves feel miserable. So you do not try to uncover the past, uncover what they did wrong, let them talk about what is going on, because that only drives them deeper into the depression, and therefore the end of the line is suicide. You do not do that kind of personalistic psychotherapy with depressives. If the gods have become diseases, then what you do in psychotherapy is feed the gods. You do not feed them their personal case history. That is, you do not go into all those ruminations that are so destructive. Rather, you go into these imaginations. You try to uncover the richness of imagination, not the personal blame and its mistakes, not the guilt but the richness of the fantasies. You feed the gods with images.

I want to read something now that comes from the book *The Rag and Bone Shop of the Heart,* which is a book of poems for men, edited by Robert

Bly, Michael Meade, and myself.[54] And though it is called poems for men, it is for diverse genders. And I am going to read you two pages written by Robert Bly as an introduction to the chapter entitled "I Know the Earth, and I am Sad."

> A man often follows or flies on an ascending arc, headed toward brilliance, inner power, authority, leadership in community, and that arc is very beautiful. But many ancient stories declare that in the midst of a man's beautiful ascending arc, the time will come naturally when he will find himself falling; he will find himself on the road of ashes, and discover at night that he is holding the ashy hand of the Lord of Death or the Lord of Divorce. He will find himself noticing the tears inside brooms or old boards; noticing how much grief the whales carry in their skulls. He realizes how much he has already lost in the reasonable way he chose to live, and how much he could easily lose in the next week. For some men, it is a time of crying in airports. "For two years, all I did, it seems to me, was cry in airports." The ashes he gets on his palm from holding hands with the Lord of Loss at night he puts on his face, and the ashes he wears will be darker than an ashy fingerprint on the forehead, even though that Catholic ritual on Ash Wednesday is so beautiful.[55]

The greatest masculine art has always been what the Romans called *gravitas*—soberness, weight, and grief. We can feel gravity when we see great art. We naturally honor *gravitas* in Rembrandt, Goya, Turner, particularly in his sea paintings, and we honor it as well in certain twentieth-century painters such as Max Ernst and Anselm Kiefer. We could say that each of these artists has accomplished, before making paintings, a descent, a fall, a drop to the floor. They have honored an agreement they could not resist, to go into grief, into *katabasis*, as the ancient Greeks called it, a drop into the underworld, that which the elevated hero Oedipus found himself undergoing. Tragedies, then, are not so much about personality flaws as they are about the depths that call up to certain men and insist they descend to.

---

54. *The Rag and Bone Shop of the Heart: Poems for Men*, edited by Robert Bly, James Hillman, and Michael Meade (New York: HarperPerennial, 1992).

55. Ibid., 95.

In our century, the Spanish and South American poets have been the masters of descent. Neruda says that he is sad because he "knows the earth." That implies that the earth itself is in grief. We can feel the sadness in the northern pines. The South Americans feel it in the rain forest and in the little towns where nothing happens:

> But above all there is a terrifying,
> a terrifying deserted dining room...
> and around it there are expanses,
> sunken factories, pieces of timber
> which I alone know,
> because I am sad, and because I travel,
> and I know the earth, and I am sad.[56]

A few years ago, in Romania archaeologists found a small basalt statue, very elegant in its blackness, of a man seated. It is the oldest Sorrowing Male found so far. It hints that grief has been for thousands of years a masculine emotion; men's sorrow seems unusual in that it seems inexplicable. Perhaps that sorrow goes back to the million or so years when men were primarily hunters. They felt the sorrow of the animal whose life they took. Or perhaps they felt the sadness of the forest. The Mediterranean world still believed at the time of Christ that there is such a thing as *lacrimae rerum*, that is, tears inside things, or tears inside nature itself. Perhaps whales and bears and oceans carry grief inside them. Ancient man lived for so many thousands of years outdoors, hunting, running, watching. And he lived in such intimate contact with animals that we can still feel in the Dordogne paintings how thin the veil was between men and creatures.[57] The sorrow of animals passed directly into men. This may be the unexplainable grief César Vallejo says comes "from the north wind and from the south wind" and is "neither parent nor son."[58]

Perhaps that is why for men depression is sometimes the entrance to soul; melancholy, a wide road to God; and ordinary grief, a door that when swung wide opens into feeling. Men often enter genuine feeling

---

56. Pablo Neruda, "Melancholy Inside Families," in ibid., 104.

57. The prehistoric paintings discovered in the Lascaux cave in 1940 in the Vézère valley in Dordogne-Périgord in France.

58. César Vallejo, "I am Going to Speak of Hope," in *The Rag and Bone Shop of the Heart*, 115.

*The Thinker of Cernavodă* (detail)
Hamangia Culture, c. 5000–4600 BCE
National History Museum of Romania, Bucharest

for the first time when in deep grief, after cheerfulness and excitement have failed for years to bring them there. Private grief can lead them to feel the sorrow of the world.

Masculine sadness, then, is a holy thing. Some men in middle age labor to find the holy stair "right to the bottom of the night."[59] It is the old god, Saturn, who presides over this dive, and it is he who knows the sadness of the huge cliffs, and the melancholy that animals feel in having to eat each other dawn after dawn, and the puzzled grief we all feel at being appointed to do mysterious tasks here, on this planet, among mountain meadows and falling stars:

> Let the young rain of tears come.
> Let the calm hands of grief come.
> It is not all as evil as you think.[60]

59. "In Memory of W. B. Yeats," in *The Collected Poetry of W.H. Auden* (New York: Random House, 1945), 51.

60. Rolf Jacobsen, "Sunflower," in *The Rag and Bone Shop of the Heart*, 111 (trans. Robert Bly).

The growth of a man can be imagined as a power that gradually expands downward: the voice expands downward into the open vowels that carry emotion, and into the rough consonants that are like gates holding that water; the hurt feelings expand downward into compassion; the intelligence expands with awe into the great arguments or antinomies men have debated for centuries; and the mood-man expands downward into those vast rooms of melancholy under the earth, where we are more alive the older we get, more in tune with the earth and the great roots. "He realizes how much he has already lost in the reasonable way he has lived." An important sentence by Robert Bly.

Theodore Roethke, who lived in Washington state, in Seattle, was a very depressed man and many of his poems express in an extraordinarily profound way the terrible condition of it and the beauty that he is able to distill. There is a poem of his called "In a Dark Time." Here are a couple of lines from it:

> In a dark time, the eye begins to see
> I meet my shadow in the deepening shade;
> I hear my echo in the echoing wood—
> A lord of nature weeping to a tree.
> I live between the heron and the wren,
> Beasts of the hill and serpents of the den.
>
> What is madness but nobility of soul
> At odds with circumstance?...

One of the most extraordinary lines you will ever find in poetry: "What is madness but nobility of soul/At odds with circumstance?"

> ...The day's on fire!
> I know the purity of pure despair,
> My shadow pinned against a sweating wall
> That place among the rocks—is it a cave,
> Or winding path? The edge is what I have...[61]

Emily Dickinson:

> I felt a Funeral, in my Brain,
> And Mourners to and fro

---

61. Theodore Roethke, "In a Dark Time," in *The Rag and Bone Shop of the Heart,* 22.

Kept treading - treading - till it seemed
That Sense was breaking through -

And when they all were seated,
A Service, like a Drum -
Kept beating - beating - til I thought
My mind was going numb -

And then I heard them lift a Box
And creak across my Soul
With those same Boots of Lead, again,
Then Space - began to toll,

As all the Heavens were a Bell,
And Being, but an Ear
And I, in Silence, some strange Race
Wrecked, solitary, here -

That word "here" is crucial. There is nowhere else, there is no escape:
"wrecked, solitary, here."

And then a Plank in Reason, broke,
And I dropped down, and down -
And hit a World, that every plunge,
And Finished knowing - then -[62]

And one more because it is so very different. About Billie Holiday. This
is from Frank O'Hara, called "The Day Lady Died," and it will probably
show more ways depression comes than any of these others I have read:

It is 12:20 in New York a Friday
three days after Bastille Day, yes
it is 1959 and I go get a shoeshine
because I will get off the 4:19 in Easthampton
at 7:15 and then go straight to dinner
and I do not know the people who will feed me

I walk up the muggy street beginning to sun
and have a hamburger and a malted and buy
an ugly NEW WORLD WRITING to see what the poets
in Ghana are doing these days

---

62. *Dickinson: Selected Poems and Commentaries,* edited by Helen Vendler (Cambridge,
Mass.: The Belknap Press of Harvard University Press, 2010), 141 (no. 340).

I go on to the bank
and Miss Stillwagon (first name Linda I once heard)
does not even look up my balance for once in her life
and in the GOLDEN GRIFFIN I get a little Verlaine
for Patsy with drawings by Bonnard although I do
think of Hesiod, trans. Richard Lattimore or
Brendan Behan's new play of *Le Balcon* or *Les Nègres*
of Genet, but I do not, I stick with Verlaine
after practically going to sleep with quandariness

and for Mike I just stroll into the PARK LANE
Liquor Store and ask for a bottle of Strega and
then I go back where I came from to 6th Avenue
and the tobacconist in the Ziegfeld Theatre and
casually ask for a box of Gauloises and a carton
of Picayunes, and a NEW YORK POST with her face on it

and I am sweating a lot by now and thinking of
leaning on the john door in the FIVE SPOT
while she whispered a song along the keyboard
to Mal Waldron and everyone and I stopped breathing.[63]

That absolute blow of loss that wipes out everything right in the midst of this ridiculous casual everyday world. "While she whispered a song along the keyboards to Mal Waldron and everyone and I stopped breathing."

Since Bly said something about Latin poets, I need to read one more. This is very clear about depression, or whatever we want to call it, this absolute terrible feeling state. "Mood" by César Vallejo, translated by Clayton Eshleman and Jose Rubia Garcia:

> I do not suffer this pain as César Vallejo. I do not ache now as an artist, as a man or even as a simple living being. I do not suffer this pain as a Catholic, as a Mohammedan or as an atheist. Today I am simply in pain. If my name were not César Vallejo, I would still suffer this very same pain. If I were not an artist, I would still suffer it. If I were not a man or even a living being, I would still suffer it. If I were not a Catholic, atheist or Mohammedan, I would still suffer it. Today I am in pain from further below. Today I am simply in pain.

---

63. Frank O'Hara, "The Day Lady Died," in *The Rag and Bone Shop of the Heart*, 109.

I ache now without any explanation. My pain is so deep that it never had a cause nor did it lack a cause now. What could have been its cause? Where is that thing so important that it might stop being its cause? Its cause is nothing; nothing could have stopped being its cause. For what has this pain been born, for itself? My pain comes the north wind and the south wind, like those neuter eggs certain rare birds lay in the wind. If my bride were dead, my pain would be the same. If they had slashed my throat all the way through, my pain would be the same. If life were, in short, different my pain would the same. Today I suffer from further above. Today I am simply in pain

I look at the hungry man's pain and see that his hunger is so far from my suffering, that if I were to fast unto death, at least a blade of grass would always sprout from my tomb. The same with the lover! How engendered his blood is, in contrast to mine without source or use!

I believed until now that all things of the universe were, inevitably, parents or sons. But behold that my pain today is neither parent nor son. It lacks a back to darken as well as having too much chest to dawn and if they put it in a dark room, it would not give light and if they put it in a brightly lit room, it would cast no shadow. Today I suffer no matter what happens. Today I am simply in pain.[64]

*Landscape and Nature*

Those are just some of the poems collected in the little chapter "I Know the Earth and I am Sad." One thing to notice is the un-caused-ness of the feeling. Another is, as Bly points out, that there are the tears in things. This is something the mystics talk about. Sophia weeping in the world. That "I know the earth, and I am sad," and that the sadness is in the earth and each part of the earth has it is own kind of sadness. You can feel that when you go out in nature at times, in places. And a curious thing happens often when we do go out in depression. We want to walk somewhere where there is a gloom that corresponds with our gloom whether it is the city streets at night, or after the rain, or the forest, or

---

64. Vallejo, "I am Going to Speak of Hope," 115.

the seashore, or wherever the places are. You can go into the redwoods and feel a terrible gloom or you can find it inspiring. I have nothing to say to that. Not every landscape is gloomy, of course, but the important thing is realizing that what you experience or what happens to you in a landscape is not your projection as psychology tells you. Because that suggests that the world is dead and un-ensouled and that there is no *anima* in the world, no animation. And as the Gestalt psychologists (not the Gestalt therapists like Fritz Perls, but the Gestalt psychologists of the 1920s and 1930s who worked out a new theory of psychology, Köhler and Koffka)[65] have said, there are physiognomic characters in the landscape. That is, there are features of the landscape like faces that reveal its own emotionality to you and correspond with human emotion.[66] *Correspond* with human emotion. That is a very important thing to realize because it suggests that the world is ensouled and what you feel out there is not merely your projection. The theory of projection suggests that you make the world, that you endow it with life, and that everything out there is simply dead matter in the Cartesian sense of simple material extension. So the emphasis on the scenes and landscapes that are in movies are on purpose. There is an enormous amount of landscapes being filmed, as well as buildings, doorways, shuttered windows, and each one of those images contains sadness, in the way Robert Bly spoke in the introduction. There are tears in those shuttered walls, in that pealing paint. Do you never feel anything sad in nature?

Now some people feel sadness, but others go out to nature to "heal." If I were nature, I'd say, Fuck you! You have destroyed me for so long that I am not going to help you with anything! We should be extraordinarily grateful for anything good that nature does for us, in light of what we have done to it. But is the same as exploiting nature for its minerals. It is almost as if we cannot get out of that box. I go to the woods to feel better when I come home, not to honor the gods of the woods. We have lost the sense that it is a living place, inhabited. And we are lucky to be

---

65. Gestalt psychology was founded in the early twentieth century by Max Wertheimer, Wolfgang Köhler, and Kurt Koffka.

66. See Koffka's *Principles of Gestalt Psychology* (New York: Harcourt, Brace and Company, 1935), 209.

able to walk in it. There is such arrogance in us to think we can use it for our own benefit. We are not that important! It is not just logging, it is the subtle attitudes we have in every way. When you take a picture of a sunset, did you ask the sunset if you can take its picture? You know, it is as if we can do anything we want with it. It is a very important reverence that is required, even for artists or therapists. I think that is what Albert Schweitzer would say, that the reverence or the awe comes first. Because if it is going to help you heal, the beginning would be a kind of propitiation of the presences that are there. Do you follow me here? This is something very dear to my heart. The subtle ways we still want to go to the jungles in order to find some medicine that we can bring back and get rid of some disease or other.

So moods are also in the landscape. There is a dark, heavy thunderstorm coming, and the landscape has this in it. There is a craggy, rocky, frozen, waterfall area with granite cliffs, and that is a mood that you read when you look at it. There is a field of daffodils, like in Wordsworth's poem "I Wandered Lonely as a Cloud," and there is a springtime mood with the beginning of the apple blossoms coming out in early May. There are moods in the landscape and the seascapes that painters did. There are endless numbers of paintings of the mood in the landscape—which is not, according to the Gestalt psychologists, a projection from the subject but is part of what they said is the physiognomic character, or the face, of what is out there in the world. This was a big step for our subjectivist psychology. Psychology since Descartes says that all subjective phenomena, all consciousness, is inside the human being and everything out there is just matter and the movement of atoms in Newton's sense. It is not conscious, it is not emotional, it is just there. Anything we see out there, we project into this inert stuff. As late as Kant's philosophy, you find that taste is not in the wine but on your tongue. There are no secondary qualities in things. There are only primary qualities in things, just atoms and their motion in space.

This kind of thinking permeated our thought for so long that it is only recently that we are beginning to admit that maybe animals have consciousness, that maybe trees have some sort of consciousness, or that there could be mood to the landscape. The Japanese, on the contrary, attribute a great deal of psychic life to places, to things, to trees, to rocks, to mountains, to streams. There are holy ones, and there are ones that are more valuable and less valuable. There are ones that are haunted or have demons, and ones that speak, and so on. For the Japanese, the discussion of their personal life and what they personally feel does not begin with an *I*. So much of our poetry is where *I* am, what *I* do, and *I* felt this and *I* felt that, and *my* father, *my* mother, and so on. Theirs is about the plum tree or something about the bamboo through the window with the snow coming down and the bending over of the bamboo. The intimate relationship between the poetics of the external world and the poetics of the internal world are enmeshed, not only because of animism—that the bamboo is experiencing melancholy—but because all things speak to each other or bespeak each other—tell about things. All things have their moods, in other words. You could see landscapes by the hundreds and every landscape is the presentation of a mood. Subjectivizing our moods, especially depression, means that we cut it from the landscape, from where it fits. A lot of the landscapes where our depressions really exist today are cityscapes, bleary, bleak, desolate, tawdry, crappy city areas—strips, bad buildings, junk, crap. Or you can go to some place that is all cleaned up like Disneyworld where it is all repressed. Now if I am not allowed to believe that there is any animistic possibility in the world around me, then that depression can only be mine—I am depressed. We do not say, "There is depression here." There is bleakness here. There is ugliness here. And I feel that. I am in that. I am in that scene. That is my set. And I could hardly expect to be different from it, unless I have developed a manic defense against it, like driving through the neighborhood with the windows up, the car doors locked, and the radio on, so that its mood does not get through to me. Then to change our moods, we go to some beautiful place. We have a *craving* for Yosemite. If only I could see a bear. Or a deer. Because I would be freed of that mood. I would get into another kind of mood. Beauty, natural beauty. So I am suggesting now that our depressions are not ours. And if they are not ours, they cannot be treated by us alone. I am following Ventura's thought in *We've Had A Hundred Years of Psychotherapy and the World's Getting Worse,* where he says that if fifty percent of the American people get divorced, that is an epidemic, or an endemic phenomenon of the culture. So how can you say that it is your fault or my fault? It is a disease or a condition of a culture—it is in the collective unconscious of the culture, so therefore there is something in the culture that is divorced or is divorcing. But our therapy, our ideations of therapy, locate all this inside the individual person and make that individual person responsible in some way for it. So, of course, you constantly feel fucked up and need more therapy.

Wanting to escape to a world that one thinks will not negatively affect ones mood. Let us go to a National Park. There are so many problems with this that I do not know where to begin. We are very much affected by realizing that our moods do connect us to places or that places give us different moods. And then the next step in the fantasy is: If I can change place, I can change myself—I will feel different. There is a great deal of truth in that, but it is not the whole story. One of the main ideas of therapy is that you do not change by getting a new wife, by moving to a new city, or by finding a new job. You still carry your problem within you. I am not sure that is entirely the case. I am not sure the American fantasy that "if I can move to Idaho, I will be all right" has not got some truth in it. Not that Idaho will make you all right, but there is truth in the idea that place is fundamental to the nature of your psyche and that we are not independent of place, that place is something constantly affecting us. Both the interiors and the exteriors that we are in have moods, and this does affect us.

I think we have learned to inure ourselves to the influence of place. If we did not, we would not be able to work where we do work, most of us. We have learned to do that whether it is hospitals or institutions or insurance offices or educational institutions. The relationship between architecture and psychology is absolutely crucial, but as long as the psyche is defined as being inside us, all that out there does not matter. But to move the psyche is definition to something more than that, even more than interpersonal relations, even more than systemic relations, family systems. To move it even further, into the relations to the furniture and into the relations of the furniture to each other in the room and so on, is so animistic and so way-out that it would take a long time for us. We would have to convert enormous numbers of our philosophic assumptions to think that way. But much of the rest of the world does think that way.

*Anger and Depression*

In the book that I have been reading from, *The Rag and Bone Shop of the Heart*, there is another chapter called "Making a Hole in Denial." These are examples of a kind of depressive anger or angry depression and how the two meet in well-executed poetry:

> When they had won the war
> And for the first time in history
> Americans were the most important people—
>
> When the leading citizens no longer lived in their shirt sleeves,
> and their wives did not scratch in public;
> Just when they'd stopped saying "Gosh!"—
>
> When their daughters seemed as sensitive
> As the tip of a fly rod,
> And their sons were as smooth as a V-8 engine—
>
> Priests, examining the entrails of birds,
> Found the heart misplaced, and seeds
> As black as death, emitting a strange odor.[67]

Louis Simpson is depressed about the state of the union, the soul of the United States, and he is angry at the same time, or at least his poem expresses that.

Another man who suffered from depression and also enjoyed anger and spleen was Mark Twain. This one is called "The War Prayer" and was written around 1904–5:

> O Lord our Father, our young patriots, idols of our hearts, go forth to battle—be Thou near them! With them—in spirit—we also go forth from the sweet peace of our beloved firesides to smite the foe. O Lord our God, help us to tear their soldiers to bloody shreds with our shells; help us to cover their smiling fields with the pale forms of their patriot dead; help us to drown the thunder of the guns with the shrieks of their wounded, writhing in pain; help us to lay waste their humble homes with a hurricane of fire; help us to wring the hearts of their unoffending widows with unavailing grief; help us to turn them out roofless with their little children to wander unfriended the wastes of their desolated land in rags and hunger and thirst, sports of the sun flames of summer

---

67. Louis Simpson, "The Inner Part," in *The Rag and Bone Shop of the Heart*, 200.

and the icy winds of winter, broken in spirit, worn with travail, imploring Thee for the refuge of the grave and denied it—for our sakes who adore Thee, Lord, blast their hopes, blight their lives, protract their bitter pilgrimage, make heavy their steps, water their way with their tears, stain the white snow with the blood of their wounded feet! We ask it, in the spirit of love, of Him Who is the Source of Love, and Who is ever-faithful refuge and friend of all that are sore beset and seek His aid with humble and contrite hearts. Amen.[68]

"Whew!" is right. Where is that language today?

The acceptance of the *gravitas*, the downward drag and sag, the increase of the melancholy disposition that comes with ageing. (It is not the only disposition that comes with age, there are other ones, too.) A little poem by Yeats. Crazy Jane is talking with the Bishop:

> I met the Bishop on the road
> And much said he and I.
> Those breasts are flat and fallen now,
> Those veins must soon run dry;
> Live in a heavenly mansion,
> Not in some foul sty.
>
> "Fair and foul and near of kin,
> And fair needs foul," I cried.
> "My friends are gone, but that is a truth
> Nor grave nor bed denied,
> Learned in bodily lowliness
> And in the heart's pride.
>
> "A woman can be proud and stiff
> When on love intent;
> But love has pitched his mansion in
> The place of excrement;
> For nothing can be sole or whole
> that has not first been rent!"[69]

Pretty good that! "But love has pitched his mansion in the place of excrement." Now if you think of that a little while, and you think of the state

---

68. Mark Twain, "The War Prayer," in ibid., 215.
69. William Butler Yeats, "Crazy Jane Talks With the Bishop," in ibid., 221.

of filth and despair that can go with depression, Yeats is saying there is love in there. Love can be found in there.

One more poem about making a hole in denial, because it is the denial of depression that one has to break through, especially in our political life. The denial of depression is very subtle now. Everything we do is so much more subtle, as if the advertising industry took over the whole thing, so that we want to discover the depression in the country, the endemic depression, so that it can be treated and it goes away. The denial is much more subtle than it ever was.

This is again César Vallejo:

Well, on the day I was born,
God was sick.

They all know that I'm alive,
that I'm vicious; and they don't know
the December that follows from that January.
Well on the day I was born,
God was sick.

There is an empty place
in my metaphysical shape
that no one can reach:
a cloister of silence
that spoke with the fire of its voice muffled.

On the day I was born,
God was sick.

Brother, listen to me, listen...
Oh, all right. Don't worry, I won't leave
without taking my Decembers along,
without leaving my Januaries behind.
Well, on the day I was born,
God was sick.

They all know that I'm alive,
that I chewed my food... and they don't know
why harsh winds whistle in my poems,
the narrow uneasiness of a coffin,
winds untangled from the Sphinx
who holds the desert for routine questioning.

Yes, they all know...Well, they don't know
that the light gets skinny
and the darkness gets bloated...
and they don't know that the Mystery joins things together...
and he is the hunchback
musical and sad who stands a little way off and foretells
the dazzling progression from the Limits.

On the day I was born,
God was sick,
gravely.[70]

So is he depressed or is he angry? Both. And there is a difference between this expression of depression and the blues. Because in the blues you have some bitterness at times, but you do not have this hardness. Mark Twain's hardness, Vallejo's hardness. You do not have that anger. At least that is my understanding and experience of it. You may have a different take on that. Country music does.

Vachel Lindsay:

Each storm-soaked flower has a beautiful eye.
And this is the voice of the stone-cold sky:
"Only boys keep their cheeks dry.
Only boys are afraid to cry.
Men thank God for tears
Alone with the memory of their dead,
Alone with lost years."[71]

Now one more. This little piece by Theodore Roethke called "The Waking." It is another poem about the feeling of melancholy:

I wake to sleep, and take my waking slow.
I feel my fate in what I cannot fear.
I learn by going where I have to go.

We think by feeling. What is there to know?
I hear my being dance from ear to ear.
I wake to sleep, and take my waking slow.

---

70. "Have You Anything to Say in Your Defense?," in ibid., 223–24 (trans. James Wright).

71. "Rain," in ibid., 102.

Of those so close beside me, which are you?
God bless the Ground! I shall walk softly there,
And learn by going where I have to go.

Light takes the Tree; but who can tell us how?
The lowly worm climbs up a winding stair;
I wake to sleep, and take my waking slow.

Great Nature has another thing to do
To you and me; so take the lively air,
And, lovely, learn by going where to go.

This shaking keeps me steady. I should know.
What falls away is always. And is near.
I wake to sleep, and take my waking slow.
I learn by going where I have to go.[72]

"I wake to sleep"—that is enough right there, "I wake to sleep, and take my waking slow."

Reading the poems was to do what we said at the beginning: clinical education. That is, to place the phenomena that you see in practice and see in your life within a nonclinical background. I want to place them within a cultural, historical, and artistic background. To give another background to the stuff that you encounter in practice and in your own life, so that you can feel that what you go through or what another person goes through is part of human existence and has a value beyond the personal. The problem with therapy, and one of the problems of the therapeutic philosophy as a whole, is that it is so individualistic. You are left somehow to carry your own life alone. It is all based on the idea that we are all individuals. We have a therapist who helps us as individuals with our individual lives. There is something wrong about this. I do not think that anyone can carry his or her life alone. Life is much too difficult to carry alone. It is a myth that we are alone. I do not think that we are alone or even that we die alone. I think the idea of "alone" is some kind of a heroic fantasy that comes out of the abandoned child fantasy. It is all part of the Moses myth, the Jesus myth, the Perseus myth, the Oedipus myth. The child is endangered, desolate, saved, and then becomes a hero. It is *one* of the myths. It is not the one we need to choose or the one we

---

72. Ibid., 381.

need to be chosen by. There are other ways of thinking. And the more we can understand that what we go through is universal, inevitable somehow, it gives it another dimension, a weight, and that is what I understand as archetypal—that it is inevitable, emotional, and universal. Universal in the sense that it happens to all kinds of people.

Also I wanted to show something about mood, the importance of mood. Depression is classically seen as a mood disorder. Now you have to understand the relative autonomy of moods—that moods come over us. They are very obscure phenomena. It is difficult to attribute a mood altogether to the brain, to hormonal or neuro-chemical physiology. It is not that there is not a component of everything we do that has a physiological aspect. There is something strange about moods. Irritability is one of them. It just comes over you. You are just doing something, and you get irritated as hell— at another driver maybe. Or you are in the post office, and there are too many people in front of you. Or somebody is talking too long to the airline clerk when you want to get your ticket. That is one of the ones I run into. And there is just this flare-up of irritability. Or horniness appears out of nowhere. All of a sudden you are horny, whether you see somebody you like or not, you are horny. Listlessness, where you just drop out and where you are not with it any more. It is not boredom, diffidence, or inattention; you are just simply listless—the current is not moving anywhere. And that mood permeates your entire day. Anxiousness can come up and be the mood. Or longing. There are an enormous number of moods, and novels are full of them, and so is poetry, and so are paintings. And the domination of one's psychic life by mood is what a melancholic person lives and feels. Mood is very, very important. Some people will not make an appointment unless they are in the right mood for whatever it is. The fact that some people can keep schedule books and tell you where they will be on January 18 at 4 pm in the afternoon *completely* independent of the mood or the weather, of the external or the internal conditions, is remarkable, if you think about it. But some of us do that—and live completely that way—and channel our moods into these little squares in our appointment book. Other people will not even make an appointment for the same day unless they can feel that they are in the right place for it. They start from the mood.

In psychology texts, when they talk about feeling, emotion, affect, and mood, mood becomes the one area that remains vague in the way it is explained and talked about. And I think that is significant, because so much of it is connected with artistic work, the riddles of artistic work, the expression of the mood, the formulation of mood, the presentation of mood. In German, mood is *Stimmung*, and *Stimmung* is connected to *Stimme* or voice, as if to say there are different voices, or a different voice speaks in the different moods. So when we say that depression is a mood disorder, we are in very vague country. We think we have said something significant, but I am not sure that we have, except that the mood level of the psyche has narrowed to a particular mood and stayed locked in that—the mood of sadness or grief or ashes, as Bly calls it. Whether it is a disorder of the mood, or whether it is the fixation on a single mood, I do not know. I only want to draw your attention to the mystery of moods.

*Imagination*

Although there is a restriction of movement and an inwardness of mood in melancholy, there is also what was called a heightened *vis imaginative*. Melancholy was the syndrome in antiquity where the imaginative powers were most activated. So though the hands are not in the world, and though the legs are heavy, and though there is impotence, constipation, and exhaustion, what goes on in the imagination is heightened. There are lots of hateful, vengeful fantasies, memories of all kinds, lewd, sexual, dirty-old-man images. There are fantasies about the bowels, high colonics, getting your rotten gut cleaned out. There are all sorts of bitter and resentful recollections about other people, which increases the repression because you are not supposed to think those thoughts. So, in one way, Saturn is supposed to feed on himself, and depression feeds on itself, because the kinds of things going on in the head are so Saturnian, so destructive, so evil, so lewd, so poisonous, so vicious, so mean, so dark, that they become more repressed. You "shouldn't" have such thoughts, which makes the depression more depressed. This is partly to explain what Freud meant when he says that the depression is due to an unconscious wish that is ego-alien, and the fear of this unconscious wish and the power of it are so great that it produces a big repression and that repression inhibits the whole being in general. This is the psychodynamic theory of it. If you think those thoughts, you are guilty of them. You should not be thinking those thoughts, so the guilt makes for even more repression.

Now my point here is that if we take it from Aristotle, and the Renaissance, that the imagination is heightened in melancholy, it makes sense that all the great writers, thinkers, and artists considered themselves melancholics. That you were melancholic indicated that you had the melancholy *furor*, an activation of the mind, even if you are sitting head in hand. Activation of the mind, even if you are thinking you are going to die any day, your mind is full of these powers of imagination, of these images. If there is no place to express them, no place to put them, no place to acknowledge them, repression increases. So one of the jobs is to let this kind of stuff appear—the pornographic craziness, the vicious murderousness, the hatreds that have been buried for a very long time, the desire for revenge. You know, revenge is a powerful emotion! It dominates seventeenth-century theater: revenge tragedies. Revenge is why Hamlet's ghost comes up, he wants revenge. Where is our revenge today? Nobody takes revenge! It is not decent to take revenge or even imagine revenge on someone. Do you realize what wonderful fantasies go on in revenge? How you can get someone, how you can fix them forever?! And hatred! So this is new age. Hatred, revenge, destruction, rot, pornography—by pornography I mean lewd and vicious fantasies as well as erotic fantasies. Also macabre fantasies, weird fantasies such as you see in movies, where the flesh is pealing off and the skin pulls apart—these are the fantasies of decay and rot and that is part of the content of what is going on in the head, part of the imagination. And as you know, the arts make a huge deal of this aspect of life. So, if we accept the old idea, going back to Aristotle, that imagination is activated most in melancholy, then what needs to be worked with in clinical depression is discovering the imagination. This ties in with the fear of suicide, because a lot of the fantasies have to do with death. Some writers say that behind all depression is the fear of death or the longing for death. If it is in melancholy, it is the longing for death. If it is in depression, it is the fear of death. Keats is full of the longing for death, Hamlet too. The romantic part longs for it, the depressive part fears it.

*Suicide*

I want to say something about suicide because the fear is, and the common wisdom is, that a person who is depressed is likely to commit suicide. That is the fear in the therapist and the common wisdom in the teaching. Meeting that suicide risk is a fundamental risk for anybody who is involved in therapy. Somehow you have to come to terms with suicide, your relation to a patient's death, and so on. It is just one of those things you have to become conscious of, otherwise you are going to become haunted and afraid because there is an undercurrent of fear at all times. The work of therapy involves terribly difficult fears, the fear of failure, the fear of the patient's suicide, the fear of the patient's violence, the fear of the law, the fear of sexual seduction—it is endless—so it is important that you have at least recognized that fear, which is right there in the room when enter.

The clinical wisdom is that you do not analyze a depression because the analysis only makes it worse for the patient and they are more likely to commit suicide. Therefore you use ameliorative measures, whether drugs or simply case management or both, but not analysis. And I think that wisdom is correct if analysis means going back into personal life history, which the patient is already doing excessively. You are going back into all of your failures, all your regrets, all the blames, all the things you did wrong with your children and all the things your parents did wrong with you, there is a sense of really being a bad person, which shows itself in the delusions of rot and appears in alchemy as the putrefaction. If it is an analysis into the personal unconscious, then it is going to exacerbate those analytical destructive thoughts and the clinical wisdom is correct. But if analysis does something else, if does not feed the disease but the god in the disease, then I would think that analysis is as important in depression as in anything else. That is, you are moving the disease from me, personally, and my obsession with my badness, into the realm of Hades, Saturn, death, darkness, mythology, gods, cosmology, metaphysics. You are deepening the thought, deepening the religion, deepening the feeling. You are doing something different than personal analysis. So it depends on what you do. If you are analyzing depression, it can go wrong. If you are deepening the melancholy, then I think that it is necessary. You may know the phrase from Jung, that "the gods have become diseases,"[73] suggesting that in all diseases there is a god and the task of the archetypal therapist is to feed the god in the disease so that the god gets more than just a disease. The god is trying to get to you through the disease, so it is the response of the therapist to bring his or her knowledge to the disease rather than following the patient's self-recriminations.

The statistics on suicide tend to be curiously gender-differentiated. Up until the 1960s, for women between 15 and 24, there were usually only three suicides per 100,000 persons in the population. That curve reached its height for women between 45 and 74 when it went up as high as 10. In other words, suicides in older women went from 3 to 10 per 100,000. When a woman was over 74, it dropped again to 5 per 100,000. So the curve is rather flat: from 3 to 10 to 5. For men, the curve was a continually ascending straight line. The older the male, the more likely the suicide. Between 15 and 24, the number was 9 per 100,000. By the time a man was 45 or 50, it was 32 per 100,000. By the time a man was 65 or 70, it was 50 per 100,000, and as he got over 75, it went up to 65 per 100,000. Whereas for a woman it had dropped to 5 per 100,000. That is an enormous discrepancy: 65 per 100,000 versus 5 per 100,000. Things have changed a bit since then. There are more suicides in younger people than there used to be, especially children. It seems that the basic curve in our country for a hundred years, up until quite recently, showed that there were very few child and adolescent suicides. Between the ages of 5 and 14 there were very few, and that has now increased considerably, especially between 15 and 24. One of the great tragedies of our American culture—I do not know about Europe—is the suicide of children. And these traditional figures are, of course, mainly for whites—so the revision of the figures is enormously important in terms of the multicultural population that we enjoy in this country.

Another aspect of suicide that is useful to think about clinically in regard to depression is that if depression is a bipolar mood disorder, meaning that there is a manic component like a yin/yang, then the suicidal moment is when the yang begins to return. That is, on the way back up and out. Getting out of it too quickly can be the manic return that

---

73. CW 13: 54.

produces the activity of the suicide—because suicide requires energy. It is the manic component that says, I can't stand it—it is the active part of the personality that cannot stand the unbearable closed-in-ness. It says that I must do something about this, I can't stand this. With the passivity of the will, absolute paralysis, the manic component is not doing anything. But once you say, I can't stand it, it is the active personality returning, and its first move is to get rid of the depression—suicide. It is the same story the Swiss tell about climbing the Matterhorn. All the accidents are on the way down. People break their legs on the way down, not climbing. That is the point of crisis, after the worst, that is when the danger is. It is the same kind of curve. It is the return of the manic—or the return of life—that is where it gets Orpheus. Orpheus is fine when he is in the underworld, it is when he is on his way back that the trouble starts. In other words, the moment you think you are over and out of it, that is the dangerous time. It is really dangerous for the clinician to think, Well, that person is no longer in danger, that person has returned to work. That is when he blows his brains out.

By the way, if you want to read a very nice little piece about depression in the early years, read A. A. Milne.[74] Eeyore is a lovely depressed figure. Remember that he gets an empty bottle for his birthday present? And a deflated balloon. See the sweetness and sadness of those images? And those belong in those tales. Eeyore is the little sad figure. How many children's books have a little sad figure? How important for the child to have little sad figures—not just Barbie dolls—or a little figure that can be sad that the child takes care of.

This leads me to also suggest the importance for clinical education of reading biographies to find some images to carry the dark days. Because biographies report how other people went through darkness. What President Johnson did during the dark days was to read Lincoln on defeat. Truman read history all the time. Montaigne, the French writer, had bladder stones and read and thought of Cicero and Seneca during his attacks. When he had bladder-stone attacks, which are very painful, he thought about ancient figures who also had similar diseases. How do you get through? How do you carry your own life? Now we have spiritual

---

74. A. A. Milne, *Winnie-the-Pooh* (New York: E. P. Dutton & Co., 1926).

ways of carrying your own life, that is, we have spiritual techniques. I am suggesting imagistic techniques. Reading biography. Having figures who help carry your life, not only your parents and grandparents. How were they when they were sick? How were they when they had cancer, and so on? This is also part of realizing that you are not alone. The sense that you are alone as an isolated individual is such a violation of the fact that we live in a community, that we are always in a community with the living and the dead. The suicide question is a pretty alive now with Kevorkian in Oregon, the Hospice movement, and the Hemlock Society.

I have been thinking about it again and I think that if a new edition of *Suicide and the Soul* comes out I would write a new postscript[75] because I think there is a mistake in the book. The book is too individualistic. I think that the old idea that a person who committed suicide had to be buried outside of the graveyard, somewhere else, not in sanctified ground, meant something that we have not understood. It was not only, as I understood it in the book, that suicide is the calling of the individual by death. But somehow it seems that we assume that suicide, the *sui* meaning self, is only yours. And I am not sure that the self is only yours. In *We've Had a Hundred Years of Psychotherapy—And the World's Getting Worse*, I tried to say that the self is an interiorization of community It is not a case of private ownership. And therefore you do not have the right to take your own life without the consent of some sort of community, whether it is the community of your family, or the community in general. It should involve some representation of community. I do not know who that community is. I do not mean that it has to be a state function, you know, that there is an office or bureau of suicide in which somebody, some social worker, comes out of there and says, Yeah, you can go. But I do think that your life is a communal affair. Because as long as it is a private right, then the self is still imagined as mine, and then we are still in individualism.

Now we have begun to talk about death, and that is, of course, a major component of the fantasy of depression, whether we are the depressed or whether we are working with the depressed. This involves us with very deep questions of philosophy and life, and so clinical education again

---

75. See Hillman's "Postscript of Afterthoughts" to the 1997 edition of *Suicide and the Soul*.

means learning a lot more than processed and managed care. Some of that withheld knowledge that John Layard said was the essence of depression[76] is the knowledge of Hades who is the god who withholds his knowledge. Nobody knows, nobody has come back, nobody can tell us. The one person who came back—Lazarus—has never said a word. It is unbelievable! The Bible left that all out! I mean here is a guy who came back! Nobody asked him anything!

There is a sentence by the literary critic Charles Glicksburg that is very important: "Twentieth-century man has ceased to believe in the reality of the invisible world. For him, there is no life after death."[77] The reality of the invisible world is one of the things the depressive is forced to notice. That there is a world that you are closed into that is absolutely real and does not allow you to go out into this world. And whether that is experienced as death or whether that is actually an entry into death or a preparation for death or a preview of death, we do not know (because Lazarus never told us.) But the reality of the invisible world is again enormously important for the archetypal therapist who is working not only with the patient's personal life but takes into consideration the reality of images. Images that are independent of the person. We do not locate those images necessarily in a person's brain or even in a person's imagination. We do not know where those images are. They do not have a *where*. They are *utopic*. Utopia means nowhere—there is no *topos*—there is no place. We do not know where they are. They seem to be attached to a place where the person is. They may even be like a guardian angel attached to a person, but the reality of the invisible world seems to be one of the important things that a therapy that goes beyond training would be concerned with. Especially in dealing with what goes on in these very dark chambers that you are closed into by depression.

Is depression part of the aging process? Is it a given that depression would come as part of the process of aging? Suppose that we were to turn

---

76. "Depression is withheld knowledge," a widely quoted phrase by Layard that appeared first as an epigraph preceding the contents page in Penelope Suttle and Peter Redgrove, *The Wise Wound: Menstruation and Everywoman* (Harmondsworth: Penguin Books, 1980).

77. Charles I. Glicksberg, *The Tragic Vision in Twentieth-Century Literature* (Carbondale: Southern Illinois University Press, 1963), xii.

that word from depression to melancholy. It seems to me that some of the most depressing moments in your life, the most melancholic moments in your life, occur in your teens. And again perhaps in your twenties and again during the midlife crisis. So, I am not sure. I think that there is a psychiatric prejudice about involutional melancholy, that we become more melancholic as we get older, more depressed as we get older. I am not sure that is right. I am not sure how to fit it with suicide statistics or any of the rest of it. I see suicide statistics having more to do with loneliness, with the separation from community, than anything else, not necessarily with mood. I see suicide more as a separation or non-adhesion into community of some kind. I am not sure of the idea that as you get older, you get more depressed. I think there are inhibitions of vital functions as you get older, but that is not necessarily melancholic or depressed.

And depression as a preparation for death? Let us remember that in our culture, if it is a manic culture, death is a stopping, and it is absolutely enraging that there should be death because it interferes with my forward motion. I have got things to do—what do you mean death?!

It is not a question of a judgment that people should not commit suicide. It is a discussion of the fact that they commit suicide. How do we understand it? Or what fantasies have we got about that? This is not a matter of ethics. It is very difficult in our culture to think about anything without first asking whether it is good or bad. We are so trained in the good-bad model that we cannot even think without putting a plus or minus sign on it. We are just talking about suicide. We have not a clue whether people should or should not do it. So what can we say about it?

The word *suicide* covers hundreds of ways of leaving this world. And in a sense, it can be extended to the fact that we are all committing suicide daily through our addictions or whatever we are doing. It becomes a dramatic act when a person takes the bottle of sleeping pills or jumps off the bridge. That is when we narrow it down and call it suicide. But the reasons that people give, the explanations, like "Fuck you, I am going to kill myself and make my parents miserable," or my husband, or wife, "they will not forget now." That is only one little box. There is another box that has to do with a desire for another world; another that has to do with the courage with which to face something; and yet another that has to do with unbearable pain. To try to collapse this extraordinary gesture into a single model is a psychological horror. If there is anything we should learn in psychology is that there are no ways of explaining human behavior. We cannot explain it. We can watch it or we can enjoy it or we can describe it. But these "Why?" questions are a disease of our Western mind. Even when you have figured out from a suicide note that this person hates his parents and that he is killing himself because he is getting revenge, there is more to it than that. And remember one thing that we do in psychology: we invent reasons for things to protect ourselves from the bare confrontation with the phenomenon. By knowing. The phenomenon is far more interesting to the soul than the reasons why. And that is why art is so wonderful. If there is suicide in art, if there is a suicide in a movie, or a play or a novel or something, it leaves you in the emotion and perplexity of it; it does not explain it. We protect ourselves with these explanations. That is partly what I am trying to do here—*not* to explain depression.

Let us go over a few things that have we have talked about today. One is the capacity to carry depression and stand in it. Another is the capacity to be communal and that one of the virtues of life is communal life. And third, that we do not have places for ritualizing grief, loss, and death. All three of those things are about not defining the self in isolation. That self is by definition cut off from other selves and has to *make* relationships. It is not inherently related. That self dominates our notions of individualism and psychotherapy. That is part of my war with psychotherapy—that it is reinforcing the modernist ego rather than deconstructing it into multiples.

Psychiatry and abnormal psychology today have to confront a new symptom. You see psyche moves through its symptoms. In the last century, we discovered hysteria and psychopathology—no one knew what it was—and from that we discovered the unconscious, repression, and all the rest. Then we moved into schizophrenia—nobody knew what that was either—and that forced the psyche to make new moves regarding images, archetypes, and complexes. Now we are discovering *multiples*. Multiples everywhere, suggesting that psyche is not a single thing but a highly dissociable group of "people," and so our definitions of things have to change. We cannot even use *bipolar* anymore, because bipolar suggests there is one thing that has two poles. But if you are multiple, you have got about nine poles or fourteen different voices, and one might be depressed, another revengeful, another a sweet little girl, and they go through different cycles at different times. So we have to get a whole new notion of the self. You yourself are a community. We have to get whole new notions of psychic reality, psychic structure. A new psychopathology is forced on us by the new movements of the psyche, the new syndromes that we are faced with, because it is the syndromes that force psychology to react with new thinking.

And to ask the person, "What do you really want?," is one of those delusions that there is a person, a single person. There is not a single person, there are multiples, there are pieces that live in the moment even when the person is killing themselves. The notion of the unity of the personality has got to be dropped. We have just got to get rid of that one so that we can free the psyche to present all its manifestations, all these things that are fundamental to human nature. We go several ways at once and at different rates of speed at once. We are now back to the issue of time. Part of us may be moving very fast while a part moves very slow. We all certainly experience how slow parts of the psyche are to realize anything, to change, and how quick other parts may be.

In depression there is a very different sense of time. One of the feelings evoked by the words "never" and "no" is endlessness. You never get to the end of it. You stay in it. It does not move. The endlessness in melancholy leads to works of eternity. Michaelangelo's, for instance. It is hard to explain this one. Endlessness imagined from the depressive point of view feels hopeless, bottomless, nowhere. If it is imagined from the melancholic point of view, then it becomes eternal. There is a big difference.

And the focus in depression is on me. The focus in melancholy—I am making these distinctions as best I can—would be on the images that are occurring to me, or on anything else. The Romantics built a lot on that kind of melancholy: walking in the woods, like poor Werther in Goethe,[78] who does kill himself in the end, but the Romantic part is fed. And if therapy remains in the narrow personalistic frame—about you and your life, you and your transference, you and your parents, or you and your

---

78. See, e.g., "Tristan, in Thomas Mann, *Stories of Three Decades,* translated by H.T. Lowe-Porter (New York: Alfred A. Knopf, 1936), p. 162: "I am a man of action. I have other things to do than to think about your unspeakable visions."

inner child—you never get to melancholy. You stay in that depressive introspection. And that leads to a suicide. That leads to a kind of hopeless despair, being trapped in the small person rather than moving into the larger person.

We discover things according to the *Zeitgeist*, and it is interesting that this all parallels the deconstruction and dismantling of modernism. As long as therapy is still concerned with building up the central ego that can cope, it is still working with modernism and has not yet moved into postmodern times. So it is still building up the modernist hero of the biography, the agent of action, like someone out of Thomas Mann.[79] Whereas deconstruction would recognize that there is no central self, there is no identity, there is no gender identity, and that is what they say. The way I see that is that you are what your communal self is at a particular moment. It depends on what community you happen to be in, which changes from time to time, and the inner world, the so-called inner world, is also a community.

Yet the difficulty is that if you retain the old monotheistic notion of Man having been created in God's image and God being one—then human beings are one in personality. Then you are always going to have a kind of senex view as to how personality has to be organized, which is central, integrated, unified, whole, and you will have the language of identity, of oneness, and so on. Now, in our time, partly in psychology but mainly in philosophy and literary criticism, the notions of self, identity, and individuality are collapsing, are being deconstructed, which allows for multiplicity, of what I have been calling polytheism. And then what appears in the psychopathology of multiples would be the way the psyche, as Jung said a long time ago, is naturally organized.[80] It is a loose association of complexes, like a group of islands or different figures, so that every dream shows you this internal drama of different figures.

Let us go back to the question of melancholy and depression. When you are depressed, something makes you go back over all these things you did wrong. It is almost as though you are a school kid having to write on

---

79. Johann Wolfgang von Goethe, *The Sufferings of Young Werther*, translated by Bayard Quincy Morgan (New York: Continuum, 1990).

80. *CW* 3: 567.

the blackboard a hundred times, "I spit on Joe Smith, I spit on Joe Smith, I spit on Joe Smith, ..." It is a kind of *iteratio,* as it is called in alchemy, a repetition—going back over and over something you did wrong. It is a self-punishment. That is a Saturnian aspect. Saturn is a punisher. Now if we turn it into Freudian language, we have a superego. If we turn it into some other kind of language, we have a punishing patriarchal father or whatever. There is a Saturnian aspect of the psyche that makes us feel guilty, that makes us repeat things again and again, that makes us feel blame-worthy, ugly, stupid.

You may think of some other things that this punishment does. It also builds something that is very important: remorse. In the language of the justice system, remorse is crucial for whether a person is imprisoned or not imprisoned, or for how long he is imprisoned. Why is remorse so important? It is a recognition of some kind of shadow. Whether it redeems you, I do not know. I do not know about redemption.

So what happens, phenomenologically, experientially, what happens when there is this kind of punishment going on? When you are punishing yourself for being such a bad person for having fucked up your life? First, by that repetition of the accusation, you develop endurance. Second, you may listen to what you have done. And third, you gain some remorse for what you have done.

*Saturn and Senex*

In alchemy, the Work was considered, at least for many, a work of Saturn. The god Saturn, who is the slowest, the farthest out, the lame one, the one who eats his children, who is oppressive, punishing, heavy, sad, and orderly, full of supposed wisdom, though I do not know what that is. I do not use that word either. I have got a whole list of words I do not use. It gets harder and harder to speak. In fact, I should make a dictionary of banned words: transformation, journey, wisdom, network, sharing, experience. Part of the job is trying to revive words that have died and let dying words go, and be able to hear when they are going. Melancholy is a good word, it is not around very much. As you know, it means "black bile," like melanoma, coal, and gall bladder. It is one of the four humors, or fluids, corresponding to the four temperaments: phlegmatic, choleric, sanguine, and melancholic. It did not mean that a melancholic temperament was necessarily clinically depressed; rather, that the melancholic temperament saw the world from a distance. It was cool and dry, laconic, quiet, hard to move, stubborn, pessimistic, anal retentive, orderly, concerned with money, clutching in the poor sense not clutching in the dependent sense, systematic. The term Saturn, or the god Saturn, also refers to a larger idea of *senex*, which was the Roman word for old man or old woman. It comes from *senes* from which we have senile, seniority, senator. The old person in the culture or the oldness of culture—things that are old.

The Work in alchemy was considered to be a *via longissima,* the longest way, suggesting that everything we do in the alchemical work, if we make that parallel to psychological work, is to be done in the longest way possible, not the shortest. When Jungians say that analysis goes on for many, many years since it is an individuation process, that is a depressing thought. It is the longest path because there are no quick solutions. The long way is the way home, not the short way. It suggests that the whole business of life is a long way—and that is the saturnine vision of life. It makes us feel that whatever retards you, holds you back, inhibits you, is a blessing from Saturn. Now that is very hard to get. Especially if you are in a manic place: your career is blocked, frustration, slowness, retardation, stupidity, failure—all those things that feel like curses—are the way Saturn blesses. Now, imagine being a god whose blessings are experienced by those who receive them as curses. In that sense, Saturn is always regarded as the cursed god. He limps, he is the god of the outhouse, the god of dirty linen and bad smells, the god of the wanderers that do not make it into the real social world. He is also the god of power in the center. It is when systems get old that they begin to belong to the senex, to Saturn. We all experience Saturn. All we have to do is look at the Senate Judiciary Committee, or at the men who speak at the Republican National Convention. And it does not have to be old men. All you have to do is look at those young men in the audience of the Republican National Convention; they are the oldest young men in America. Saturn, the senex, is a style of thinking and style of life in which "No" is a very important word. And which includes order, time, endurance, feeling oneself out of it, being excluded. It is the planet that is far out, on the edge. Now when those experiences hit us—being on the edge, excluded, not making it, being frustrated—we feel it as a curse. We do not realize that when these things are gone into in depth, they are actual blessings that give weight to the psyche. They give *gravitas*, depth, keep lead in the keel. So when you look back on your life, you often realize that those places where you were blocked, frustrated, burdened, depressed, that have been frustrations at the time, also added weight to your psyche.

Something more is there because of what Saturn has done to you. It is a realization that took me a very long time. I was standing outside the Temple of Saturn in Rome[81] when it hit me, that all these things that I had complained about as curses were actually the way Saturn reaches you. Do you see what I am saying there? He does not reach you with Mercurial gifts or Venusian gifts. He reaches you through the things that feel like oppressions, wrongs, punishments. The sense that the sad things are not just deprivation and loss but also a gift comes to us in the word *gravitas*. It means grave, to be serious, but it also has the same root as the word *gravid*, which means pregnant. Or in English, the word "sad" has a root in the Old English *sæd*, which meant "full, satiated." They used the word after a big dinner to mean that they were sated, satisfied, full. So you can be full of sorrow, filled with tears, and that is something that we do not realize enough. Loss is not quite as empty as we tend to think. Actually when you have lost something dear and beloved, you are filled with that loss. It is not quite the same thing as being hollow or void. You use the word "nothing" for empty, for vanity. There is a fullness that comes with a full immersion in the Saturnian depression or melancholy.

The job is to become aware of the language and to turn the language. Turn it all the time. For example, this question of the cursing of Saturn. If you have your horoscope done, one thing they will usually tell you about is that Saturn does this, or restricts you here, if you have the Moon and Saturn in the First House. It can mean all kinds of things that are very negative. How can you experience your curses as blessings? That is turning the Saturnian. And that is also a way of realizing what a poor cursed god he is. No wonder he is the god of outcasts, exiles, beggars, and people with crutches. He is the god of all that because his blessings are always understood as curses, so he is cursed by this. That is the curse

---

81. The ruins of the Templum Saturni stand at the foot of the Capitoline Hill at the western end of the Forum Romanum.

on him, of not being understood. What he offers is not accepted, so he is an outcast at the far edge of the system. So it is a mode of trying to get hold of the curses in your life. And therapy must make that move. It must move all those pieces of childhood that you feel are cursed into realizing the blessing in the curse. So that you no longer can distinguish a blessing or a curse: I mean that is the real move—you cannot call it good or bad. It *is*. That is the realism that Saturn also brings.

We have lots of models in mythology for the ordinary experience of depression. One of them is the Christian one. That is the Garden of Gethsemane, the unbearable burden: "Let this cup from me."[82] Peter not answering, betrayal, the cross, the horror of the cross with the torture and the vinegar and the thorns, and so on. But two days later, resurrection. And that model dominates our thinking about depression in our culture. There is light at the end of the tunnel—hang on and you will come out alright at the other end. There will be a new day. It is bad now, but it will get better. So that is one model: down and back up. That is a mythical model, one of the myths that tells us how we experience depression. A friend of mine pointed out that rather than thinking of the crucifixion as the model, perhaps we should look at simply the descent into the human world—the limitation of incarnation would be the state of melancholy. Being here seems the hardest thing of all.

But there are lots of other mythological models for depression. If we ask which god is in the disease, then the problem is, which god are we thinking of? Which god appears in the disease? How does one recognize the myth in the disorder? In the story of Demeter, her daughter is carried off, raped, carried away, dragged into the underworld by the god of death, by the invisible god of darkness. And Demeter goes into a tremendous depression. She sits down. She will not move. She mourns. She rages. She will not eat. All the vegetative world stops. She will not laugh. She will not smile. She will not let the green world begin again, and only through some trick of Baubo and some dirty images—very important again, the pornographic aspect—she comes back to life.[83] The gods bring her back to life, even though she at first refuses everything.

---

82. Matthew 26: 39.
83. Baubo causes Demeter to laugh by exposing her genitals; Orphic Fr. 52.

That is another kind of myth: a myth of loss. And it is not the same as a descent into the underworld and coming back up again as with Christ and the weekend—Friday to Sunday—resurrection. It is very long, dragged out, and desperate in the Demeter myth, and I think that is extremely important to realize. The myth was the central myth of the Greek world in the Eleusinian mysteries to which all the citizens went and took part in. They were shown something about the depths of the soul. They were not shown a quick resurrection fantasy. And they were not shown torture and betrayal, as in the Christian story. They were shown the loss of a daughter, of a soul being taken to the underworld as a necessity. So you see, you have different mythical backgrounds against which to put the experiences you have. That is the value of having different myths. Then you can see differently. It is not about which myth is right. But if you think along the Christian lines or if you think along the Demeter lines, what are the results, what does it do for you, how does it set the thing up? Certainly, if you think along the Christian lines, you are expectant of a better state to come, with resurrection and redemption to follow.

Dionysus is another model of being pursued, haunted by enemies, and taking flight by going down. If you remember your own dreams, how many times have you been pursued and where do you go when you are pursued, what is the sanctuary? Very often we go up. Climb a tree, run upstairs. All those movies where the guy is being pursued and he goes up to the roof to escape. Well, Dionysus goes down to escape. He goes into the underworld, or he goes to the bottom of the sea, or he is pulled apart into all directions. I think that is important. Osiris is also pulled apart in all directions—his whole body is pulled apart. So that again gives a different experience of being destroyed by depression. And in the Dionysian myths, there were celebrations called *tristia* and *hileria. Tristia* was the time when the god was gone and the world was sad, *triste.* And when the god returned, *hileria* started, a hilarious, joyful, exciting time. It was a cycle that was connected the god's nature of coming and going. It was not anybody's responsibility. It was followed the movement of the god's energy.

We need to deepen ourselves by going into the Saturnian world. I think that withheld knowledge is the knowledge of Saturn and Hades. It is a knowledge of melancholy, so that we can feed the god in the disease and not the disease. But I do not want to put all depression with Saturn or all the depression with Hades. There is a Demeter depression. And there is a phase of Hera's life (she had three phases in her life). In the third, she is called the Left One, the one who is left, so that in the phenomenology of marriage, there is always the emotion of being deserted. It belongs to Hera, and try not to hear this in a feminist way, within the phenomenology of marriage. She is the goddess of the mating instinct. There is always the feeling that you are being left behind. That is a depressive, paralyzing, and shattering feeling—that you will be left, that you are left, that you have been left. Your mate is elsewhere, and you are alone. It may have nothing to do with your mate. It belongs to the phenomenology of the myth.

Another god or goddess that also has a depressive side is Mars. Old Mars in some of the ancient images is a rusty, cynical, isolated figure, encased in iron armor, or living in a tower. Some of the images of Mars show a tower or an old man covered in armor. That rusting, bitter, isolated, curmudgeonly, martial depression is a phenomenon you see in older men very often. Rusty, bitter, alone. If I spend a lot of time on Saturn or Hades, it is not to say that this is the only way it works or that these are the only gods involved. But Saturn has a particular role in our myths, in our Western literature and painting of the old, the depressed, and the isolated.

These mythological views suggest alternative models for your experiences. This is what I mean by polytheistic psychology. The different complexes can be imagined in different styles. They do not all have to be imagined in the same uniform way. And you do not know quite which way it is going to go with you.

Sometimes alchemy was called the mysticism of Saturn. Now this is a way of giving to those times of depression in your life a different kind of value. Of recognizing that somehow the soul needs to go through this. You do not need it, you do not want it, and you would rather buy a new car, but the soul needs to go through this, and we do not know why. Maybe it is to add weight, maybe it is because of karma. Saturn was the god of karma too. The ancestral curses came down on you through Saturn, and the ancestral blessings. Something needs to be lived this way. The reason that the alchemical vision of lead was banned by the

Pope[84] in 1317—alchemy was no longer to be practiced, but it continued to be ever since—was that it invited the melancholy of loneliness. It was regarded as a melancholic occupation. You see one of the reasons it was banned was that it was anti-communal. Now that is again an interesting thought because the Church always said that by being in the Church, you were in the body of Christ, and you were in the community. The Church had this communal idea from the very beginning. One of the reasons they said alchemy was not good for you was that it made you do your own thing. Therefore, it produced depression and paranoia. They also banned it because it was greedy—it tried to make gold. It was also banned because it had astrological importance, and the Church was not in favor of astrology, which suggested predestination rather than prayer, works, and staying within the Church and doing the sacraments, and so on. When I say "the Church," you have to realize, whether you like it or not, whether you practice it or not, whether you have any notion of it at all, that we are all Christians. Christianity has been around for two thousand years, and you cannot escape it. You can become an atheist, you can become a Jew or a Muslim, you can do all these things, but you cannot escape the fact that you have got two thousand years of it in your wiring. So when I refer to what "the Church" thinks or what "the Church" says, it is what is going on in your own psyche because it is going on in the culture.

Now, they had a lot of words in the Middle Ages for melancholy. They had *sicitas*, which was dryness; they had *pigrethia*, which was sloth; they had *desidia*, which was a complete paralysis; and they had *acedia*, which was a very bad thing and among the seven sins. *Acedia* means torpor, lack of interest, indifference to the spiritual: "I could not care less." It appeared in a monk when he did not go out and do the field work, when he did not get up at four in the morning and do his prayers, when he did not work in the bakery, when he did not work in the vineyards, when he had no interest in praying, no interest in ritual, no interest in the spiritual life. In our language: he was depressed. This was a very serious matter. A lot has been written about it. And it was different than just being sad,

---

84. The papal decree *Spondent quas non exhibent* (sometimes referred to as *Spondent pariter*), promulgated in 1317 by Pope John XXII, forbade the practice of alchemy.

different than being *tarditas,* which was being late, or being *somnolant,* falling asleep during prayers or during services, or *oteum,* being bored, or *tepitas,* being tepid about things, just take it or leave it. You see the desert saints who started the monasteries, who are the background of all our ascetic ideas—the more spiritual you get, the less meat you will eat, and all the rest—the whole asceticism that runs through the culture, whether it is the asceticism of actual religious practices or the asceticism of vitamins and jogging, and so on, this ascetic craziness that infects the United States, has behind it the desert saints. The desert saints were called *athletes*—the athletes of God. It was a heroic fantasy. You were to stay awake, you were not to dream, you were not to sleep. And, of course, *acedia,* this torpor, this lack of interest, falling asleep, not caring, and all these words I have listed for you, sloth and dryness and lack of interest, somnolence and being late, all of these, of course, do not fit an athlete of God. They are not Herculean, not heroic. So we have a long history against the depressive part of nature. It is not only the images of Christ or St. George or Mary standing on the dragon or serpent, the earthy muddy part of life. It is also something to do with the inertia, the downward pull. And that downward pull is what returns again and again in depression and melancholy. That is why, as we were saying before, women have been carrying it. Because in the Church's mind, women are the embodiment of the earth and water elements, the lower elements. So by talking about depression today we are also part of this whole question of re-evaluating what is popularly called the ecological, the feminine, nature, the earth, the goddess, and so forth. The trouble is, all those good words, the goddess, the feminine, the earth, the ecological, never bring in the pathology, the depression, that goes with it. If you are going to get in touch with the downward movement, you are also going to get in touch with depression and melancholy. That is the door, maybe, to it. And that is fundamental to archetypal psychology, that whatever is going to enter, enters through the door of pathology. The doors are wide open, they do not even revolve, they are just there. "Come on in, it is fun," the New Age, whatever. Archetypal psychology tries to remember that everything is pathological. That is what it is all about.

Now here is a very basic question. Should we believe in the reality of these animated forces in our lives or not? I do not know. When I speak of them as descriptive tools, as images against which we can imagine and think, that is one way of imagining them. But if I speak of them in another way, as powers, I use the term "as if." If I hypothesize them as powers, then I can create graven images, idols. And they may be. We do not know. They exist in myth. Myth is not theology. Theology has to create belief. These gods do not ask to be believed in. They ask to be remembered. You remember them by telling stories, by talking about them, reading about them, looking at images of them. That is one big difference: you do not have to believe in them. The second big difference is, there is no holy text. There is no authentic way to talk about any of them. There is an authentic way to talk about the God of the Old Testament and the God of the New Testament because it is written. Now everybody argues about it, and there are, especially among the Jews, hundreds of different ways of understanding the Bible, but it is written. In the Greek world, the Roman world, or the mythological world, there is no book religion, so you do not have any text, and you cannot ever go really wrong. You have stories, plays, images, and poems.

It is not that the gods are made up by the human psyche. The mythological viewpoint is that they precede the human psyche. They are the *a priori* of the human psyche in the way that Jung speaks of archetypes. They are prior to in *value,* not necessarily prior to in time or prior ontologically, at least in the way I read it. If you start to say they are prior ontologically, then their existence would be prior to our existence, and the n you've hypothesized them. I make the gods prior in value, while a humanist would make the human prior in value.

Psychic reality is real. Of course, "real" is not necessarily meant in a literal sense; it just means that if you think a thought, that is a real thought, then you have thought a thought. If you have a fantasy or a dream, that is real. It is not a lie, not an illusion. We tend to think that real means concrete: *That!* It is very difficult to know how to keep them as imaginal reals rather than as theological reals or philosophical reals or religious reals, because we do not have the sense that the imagination is utterly real. It is a difficult thing to contemplate, and we tend to jump into belief very quickly. It is like the figures in your dreams. Where do they go when you wake up in the morning? And what do they do the rest of the day? As long as we think they are part of us and in our heads, then they are turned off, and when we go to sleep at night, then we turn them back on. But that is questionable.

Do I think the soul has a need to believe? Sure, the soul has a need to believe. But I am wary of belief because it is a bedrock of Christianism, of the Credo. The Greeks did not ever say that. They did not even have religion. They had stories, rituals, practices, and holy places. They did not *believe* the owl was Athene. When the owl hooted at night, it was Athene; it was not a question of belief. You see our God because he is not physical, visible, or tangible. The only way we know he is around is if we believe in him. The Greeks did not ask to believe in their gods, because they were present in everything. Aphrodite was in a clamshell. Athene was in an owl's hoot. Apollo was in the sunrise. They were concrete, sensual presences. You do not believe in a tree; you see it. But if God is invisible, transcendent, immaterial, then you have to believe in him. How else are you going to know he is around? So *that* god asks for belief. The Greek gods did not ask for belief. Belief is a very difficult thing. A delusion is called a false belief in psychiatry, in psychopathology. How do you know when a belief is false? If four people agree to the same delusion, is it a false belief? The people in Jonestown who drank the Gatorade, were they deluded or in a religious belief system?[85] We do not know. You cannot establish belief. You cannot solve the problem of false belief. If enough people believe in it, it is no longer a false belief.

The soul is a sucker for belief. The soul goes for it. And as Heraclitus said, "Dry, the soul grows wise."[86] I do think that the soul wants to be inspired by spirit, and it does long to go beyond itself. What I am arguing about is the folly of our Western culture in constantly believing in something, whether it is Pepsodent toothpaste or the end of the world. We are very naive. Our beliefs keep us very naive. Can you live without belief, recognizing that the soul is always eager to believe? At the same time that the soul is eager to believe, can you live with that open realization that is a psychological insight into belief so you do not fall for it? One

---

85. The Jonestown Massacre, where more than 900 people, many of them children, died in a mass murder-suicide in 1978 by drinking a cyanide-laced punch at the order of cult leader Jim Jones.

86. Fr. 74. Heraclitus, *Fragments,* translated by Brooks Haxton, with a foreword by James Hillman (New York: Penguin Books, 2001), 47.

gift of depression is that we are knocked below our beliefs. It does knock the props out from whatever system has held you up. Part of the loss is of whatever it was holding you up.

I am going to read some passages from something I wrote some time ago, "The 'Negative' Senex and a Renaissance Solution,"[87] just to give you some feeling for this senex quality that is within melancholy:

> Alchemy says how this work proceeds: "The divine organ is the head, for it is the abode of the divine part, namely the soul..." and the philosopher [meaning the alchemist] must "surround this organ with greater care than other organs."[88]

When you call something a head-trip you are neglecting the head, you are not surrounding the head with greater care. Now, to surround the head with greater care means to take great care with what thoughts go on and where you put your head and how you care for your head and what things you let into your head. See, to dismiss the head by saying that someone is merely on a head-trip—which in many cases is filled with academic concepts, TV trivia, or second-rate fluff—suggests you need to think well, carefully, considerately, or with sensitivity. When the darkening of the soul speaks, it has its own voice.

This is a passage from one of these old alchemical texts. It begins,

> I am an infirm and weak old man, surnamed the dragon; ...

If you live with a person seriously depressed, that person feels like a dragon. They consume all the air around you and the air stinks. You want to get away from them because their depression eats everything up.

> therefore I am shut up in a cave...A fiery sword inflicts great torments upon me; ...

That fiery sword can be the self-punishment, can be the attacks you make on trying to end this state. The fiery sword is the acute attitude.

> death makes weak my flesh and bones...My soul and my spirit depart; a terrible poison, I am likened to the black raven...; in dust and earth I lie.[89]

---

87. *Spring: A Journal of Archetype and Culture* (1975): 77–109. Reprinted in *UE 3: Senex & Puer.*

88. *UE 3: Senex & Puer,* 254 (cited by Jung in *CW* 14: 732).

89. Ibid., 255 (cited in *CW* 14: 733).

The black raven being one of the birds of doom; the owl is another bird of doom, which sometimes appears in dreams or in lore and fairy tales to repeat doleful sayings. Everything's getting worse, there is no hope, there is no way out of this, I have fucked up my whole life, there is no place to go from here, I cannot get it together and so on. I remember a woman once in analysis with me in Zurich who dreamt of dark glasses that had a frame made of raven wings. She would come in and say, again and again, "Es wird immer schlimmer"—it is getting worse and worse, it is getting worse and worse. She was seeing the world through the raven's view. She was making prophetic announcements about darkness and doom.

> Senex destructiveness [the Saturnian destructive side] confronts us more dangerously than we realize...

Now I am talking not about the emotion of depression but its mental set.

> particularly when we fasten attention on destruction elsewhere, e.g., the violent and aimless chaos of youth.

There is nothing that the senex enjoys more than seeing gangs in LA being destructive, seeing the people running in and out of the stores looting, because this projects destruction away from the senex onto others—violent youth, criminal youth, other races, and so on.

> The danger from the senex lies just in the fact that we are unaware of it as dangerous.[90]

Who would think Scowcroft was dangerous?[91]

> We are so used to the institutions of order into which we mold our society, our lives and conceptions, we do not see that these institutions and images are patterned after a senex God and are conditioned by senex forces. We are so used to our complexes and their odors that we do not realize their decay.[92]

If you live in your own stink long enough, it does not smell any more. So we do not notice what we exude from our white culture. We do not know about our own white ghetto because we live in it.

---

90. Ibid., 256.

91. Brent Scowcroft was United States National Security Advisor under Presidents Gerald Ford and George H.W. Bush.

92. UE3: *Senex & Puer*, 256.

Within ourselves, the senex fights to maintain order by laying down the law or projecting some new system to end conflict.[93]

During the [1992] election, the senex appeared in all three candidates[94] trying to show some new system that would end the problems. That is an appeal to the senex thinking: new order, new law, new system.

I want to tell you about one very classic image of the old man: the melancholic old man in the tale of the Roman Charity (*Caritas Romana*) or Cimon and Pero. It was painted by many artist in the Renaissance, and after.[95] It is an image of an old man locked into a prison cell. He is down in a dungeon and there is a little bit of light coming in from above, and his daughter visits and gives him her breast milk. Now that is a metaphor, a very powerful metaphor of depression that caught the imagination of Renaissance and also Dutch painters. Imagine that this old man is in every person: old, depressed, unable to move, locked into a system, locked into habits, locked into prejudices, locked into the belief systems that have become prejudices. It is cold, it is damp, and dark in that world. Now what comes in to give milk? This was supposed to be something that young Roman matrons were to do, to visit prisoners.

The Roman note of *caritas*, charity toward the imprisoned, is also to be expanded to giving the milk of human kindness to the depression, and tenderly taking care of what goes on in the head. So the idea of self-punishment is moved now to finding a soulful way of taking care of the depression. That may make it slowly move, soften, weaken, and be nourished, because milk is also food of the imagination. It is the holy food of the gods, the holy food of the child, the holy food of the prophet and the saint, and so on. It is the milk that is both imagination and kindness or sweetness: charity. And that may move the depression from black to blue. Because that is all the movement one might think is possible. Because in alchemy it would be the movement from black to blue, blue being the

93. Ibid., 258.

94. In 1992, Ross Perot was running for president against President George H.W. Bush and the Democratic nominee Bill Clinton.

95. First painted in Germany by both Barthel and Sebald Beham, then in Italy by Caravaggio and Artemisia Gentileschi. Rubens is known to have painted at least three versions. Poussin included it in his *The Gathering of the Manna* (1639).

Hinc pater hinc natus, Charitas me impellit vtring:
Sed prius hunc seruo, gignere quem nequeo.

J. Pesne fecit

Poussin Inuenit                    Le Blond Exc                    Auec Priuilege du Roy

Jean Pesne
(after Nicolas Poussin)
*Charity*, before 1669
Etching

capacity to sing the depression rather than to be in the depression. The capacity to imagine the depression rather than to be only depressed. If you think about the blues, if you think about country music, it is nearly all about loss, loneliness, betrayal, desertion, fucked-up-ness. The great lament that goes through our country is expressed in the western country songs and in the blues. That is where you can hear it. And that is the movement from the black to the blues. That is the movement from identification with lead, or with being poisoned by lead as the alchemists said, to the expression of loss and regret.

One of the old ideas of the blue in Sufi mysticism was that apprentices wore blue. At a certain time, they changed colors. They wore blue in remembrance of what they have lost. Part of the blueing of the psyche is remembering what you have lost; it is nostalgia. That is a melancholic condition. It is not so bitter. Where did it all go? At the moment that you can think, Where did it all go? you have the images of how it once was. You have those images of love. You have those images of beauty. You have those images of poetry. You have those images of people, beloved people, those scenes, those moments. And that is nostalgic and sad, but not the same as having no images. That is the milk flowing a bit. There is beauty in that. And that is something moving from the black to the blue, moving from depression to melancholy, because beauty comes in, some kind of poetic beauty, like the beauty in music. Listen to Beethoven's last quartets, to Mahler, to Sibelius, where there is terrible pathos, terrible sadness, and at the same time, there is a melancholy beauty that is terribly moving to the soul as though the soul craves that. It may long for belief, but it may long for beauty even more. In fact, if it found some beauty, it would not need to believe in anything.

I think we should not think only in terms of moving towards blues. We still have to be immersed in the black. And the need for that is so strong all you have to do is walk up to the Viet Nam memorial and you can feel in that black wall how powerfully we need something. Let alone Iraq, we are still in the 1960s. And there are probably many more things that need mourning. Many, many more things. Once we begin to remember the 500 years since Columbus landed, it is a history of extermination. And it goes on continuously, if not in the United States, it goes on in other places with mahogany forests and dead fish, and whatever it is. Somalia.

Imagine that we cannot get it together to do something about Somalia! We could get it together in four days to get to Kuwait.

There is so much to mourn or to feel about, which maybe is the reason why we are so hyper-manic. The entire culture is in a manic denial—a successful manic denial. There are not really any rituals of mourning or loss. The last few wars could be remembered. There is a great deal of destruction even within our own culture that could be remembered. We could remember Three Mile Island once a year. I mean there is endless things to remember. We remember them with manic displays. Yellow is the brightest color, an Apollonic color. That is what we wore for the Iraq massacres. And the wounded in that war were not allowed to parade down Fifth Avenue in New York.

There is a great deal that could be mourned. And I am a little cautious about inventing rituals. I think the longing for rituals should be experienced very fully. The sense of not having it, the sense of loss, should be felt so strongly that something will emerge from that. We in America tend to look for solutions before we have felt the problem. Let us just feel the problem for awhile. The absence, the longing, the need, and then see what the psyche presents.

So depression, I say again, is a subject that needs to be talked about when we talk about feminism, when we talk about ecology. When we talk about any of these subjects, we must lift the repression from the depression. When depression comes individually into your life, it may not be your fault, your personal mess-up, but because you are carrying a piece of the collective psyche. Jung made it very clear that we are all in the collective unconscious. Michael Ventura says in the book *We've Had a Hundred Years of Psychotherapy—And the World's Getting Worse,*[96] that if fifty percent of marriages end in divorce, then it is a collective endemic disease. You cannot solve that alone in your relationship. It is endemic, it is in the culture. Many of the problems, including depression, are in the culture.

The task, first of all, is to realize the importance of the depressive moments in your life. They are important for the individual soul and they are important for the collective soul. The more one can absorb those moments of melancholy, the more possibilities there are for relief. And

---

96. Hillman and Ventura, *We've Had a Hundred Years of Psychotherapy,* 54.

also, possibly, for finding more beauty. Two things that I think are very important for the culture are slowing down and finding beauty. But I do not think you can abstractly decide which part of it is yours and which part is the society's.

There are other ways of imagining all this. The idea of Sophia, the feminine figure of wisdom is one. Or that the world is in the original sin, and therefore everything is unhappy. And we are waiting for the redeemer. You see, all of these systems are available to us, metaphysical explanations of why there is sadness. My job is just to remind us that we do not know why there is sadness. But there is. And we need to take an interest in sadness.

Now, the very fact that we are using the language of loss means we are back into our box. We are back in the room of depression when we are talking about loss. But we wonder how long we should grieve. What is excessive grieving? Again, there is this notion of balance. We are very much afraid of too much of anything. So we have recovery groups of all kinds. Too much sex, too much eating, too much... And this gets us back to Saturn.

Saturn is a master of discipline. And master of certain disciplines like mathematics and geometry that are very rigorous and disciplined. In the old lore, they belonged to Saturn. He is also the master of another kind of discipline, that which grants endurance of pain. He was the punisher, but he was also the god of punishment in the sense that you would turn to Saturn to endure the punishment. And the question of sadism goes with that. Saturn has to do with counting and numbers. Saturn has to do with the mint. He did not invent the mint, but he is the god of minting money and counting. Now there is an interesting connection because in sadistic practices, as for example in the Marquis de Sade, you get forty-two lashes or twenty-one, whatever it is, all measured and counted. And there is something extremely oppressive about having to deal with an accountant, like your tax accountant, having to deal with anybody who takes exact measurements. You can feel the Saturn effect and the delight that some people take in it. Great delight in finding two pennies wrong on the balance sheet, balancing the checkbook, figuring it all, and the oppression that can come in a marriage between the one who balances the checkbook and the one who does not balance the checkbook and how that can be used as a sort of Saturnian oppressive dictatorship of discipline. So this is part of Saturn's way of working, but this is outside of the realm of depression. This is part of Saturn as a whole. Saturn covers lots of other things besides melancholy and depression.

The discipline is not necessarily depressive for people who are, as they used to say, children of Saturn. It is enjoyable. It is what the Freudians say: the anal retentive *enjoys* all those aspects of anality. It is a pleasure to say, No I don't want any more cake. I'll only have one portion and watch everybody else go greedy. That is an anal pleasure.

Let us also not forget that depression is one of the main humors—and I do not mean the humors in the temperament sense, I mean jokes. Black humor as it is called, gallows humor, bitter, ironic, sardonic humor is an entire realm of jokes and humor that belong to the saturnine way of looking at the world. That is another aspect. You see, each of these gods has his own rhetoric and has his or her own forms of laughter, forms of humor, forms of everything. It does not mean you have to be humorless to be Saturnian. Satire! In fact, the words satire, saturnalia, and Saturn are all part of the same root. Saturnine Night Live! It is on Saturday night also. It got a little bitterness in it too.

Saturn is returning in our culture. We may be, as some have said, an always youthful, adolescent culture, a puer culture, a heroic culture, going always with our manifest destiny. But now we are voting for 100,000 cops on the streets, and for more and more prisons. Prisons belong to Saturn. More and more, there is greed and the eating of children. Saturn eats his own children. There is more and more anxiety about toxicity. Saturn was also a god of the shithouse, the outhouse, of poisons and foulness. And I think political correctness is a Saturnian kind of thing. It keeps things in straight lines. Also all the litigation and the attempt to settle things by judgment, not by harmony, not by consensus, not by persuasion, but by judgment. We must have nine old men decide things for us. (I include the two women on the Supreme Court as part of the nine old men.)

So Saturn returns, and how do we deal with it? I think we need to know a little more about the archetypal word, *senex. Senex* is the Latin word for the old man or the old woman. It corresponds to *puer,* which is the young boy, the youth. The word still appears in senile, senator, senescence. It refers to the last phase of life, to winter. The way the lore

PART TWO: THREE SEMINARS / 131

describes the senex figure or the senex archetype is that the temperament of the senex is cold, which can also be expressed as distanced, outside of things, lonely, wandering, set apart, outcast. The coldness also of cold reality: things just as they are, dry data, unchangeable, cold, hard facts. And coldness is cruel without the warmth of hearth and heat of rage, but full of slow revenge, torture, exacting tribute, bondage. These are some of the feelings you have in dark depressions—that something is torturing you, that you are being tortured, imprisoned, impoverished, in bondage to it. As lord of the farthest out, because Saturn was considered the most way-out planet—before the discovery of Uranus, Neptune, Pluto—Saturn was the farthest away of all things. He views the world from way outside. So there is an enormous perspective in all this. One of the things that depression does is relieve you from involvement so that you get a new kind of distance and some new insights. A distant view of things, so that eventually, possibly, you see the structure of things. And, therefore, one of the emblems of the senex is the skull, suggesting that everything can be envisioned from its death aspect. What is the essential thing going on here? What is the ultimate psychic core once all the dynamics, psychodynamics, and explanations are gone? What is the final view of something?

Slow and heavy, chronic and leaden, these qualities refer to Saturn. Lead was especially important to the alchemical work of redemption. You see, the different planets were associated with different metals. Each of the seven planets had a metal, and every one of the metals was in the earth and formed the substance of our lives. Copper belonged to Venus; lead, to Saturn; mercury, to Mercury; gold, to the Sun; silver, to the Moon. They talk about lead in the old texts, even used lead concoctions in the medicine of the seventeenth century. They used to make medicine out of lead. Today we know what lead does, but they made medicine. I have a little book called *The Concoctions of Lead,* which lists recipes for how to make lead tinctures for people. When you look at it carefully, it is interesting to see that these concoctions were used for ailments that would follow the saturnine type. They were used for joints, rheumatics, hemorrhoids, skin ulcers and cancers, and in most of these concoctions, lead is to be concocted with vinegar.

In the alchemical work of soul-making, the lead appeared at the beginning and also at the end, suggesting a certain quality of consciousness, a certain heaviness, weightiness, gravity, density, and softness. Lead is the softest of metals. It melts most easily, its melting temperature being lower than copper or silver. These qualities made soul: weight, density, solidity, and softness. So that is why it was the beginning of the work and the end of the work. At the beginning of the work, you get the oppression. Nothing works anymore, you are stuck, your life is not flowing. It is not going anywhere, the soul is stuck. It begins in lead. At the end of the work, you get the capacity to be heavy, the ability to have weight, to have ponderousness, to be able to ponder, to weigh things, to sink down. And there is something else about lead that is very important. When you are in a depression, you cannot see anything. You have no insights. All you can do with lead is bear it, feel its weight. It is very interesting, before we had digital publishing, print was set in lead. What we read on a page was put there by lead. I do not know if that makes our old books heavier or more serious or whatever, but there is a very big difference between spraying a jet of ink on a page and pressing a piece of lead onto a piece of paper. If you have ever seen an old printing press with great big hunks of lead, and how lead was poured into a mould and then set into words. Pretty impressive. Im-pressive, yes. It was a quality of consciousness that the alchemist had to have inherently present as a model of soul-making in order to do his work. He had to be in his own way a melancholic temperament in order to be slow enough to do the work. I think all this bears very much on the practice of therapy.

The ending in Saturn—of course, I am still in the middle, so I have no idea what the end is like—but my guess is that it has something to do with the utter weightiness, the indestructible reality—what word can I use—of the soul, of the psyche. It is similar to seven chakras, the energy centers of the body. The first, the root chakra, is an elephant, a big heavy elephant. So that would be beginning in Saturn, to make a parallel, and then there is the throat chakra, which is also an elephant. Now, of course, Kundalini goes further,[97] but let's just stay with the chakras, with the place of the complete reality of the word. The complete reality of the expression of the throat, of psychic reality. I think that is part of what ending in Saturn is.

---

97. See Hillman's "Commentary to *Kundalini: The Evolutionary Energy in Man* by Gopi Krishna," in *UE 7: Inhuman Relations*.

All of the things you have been through are built into the psyche in a leaden way, and you have stopped seeing through. The important thing about lead is that nothing gets through it. That is why when you are in a depression, you cannot understand it and you cannot see through it. We put lead over us to prevent the X-rays from coming through, we put lead around plutonium. Lead is the heavy, dense, impossible metal, a super metal. That incapacity to see through, to understand, to know: lead blocks all that. There is no insight at all, you are just in it. That the work ends in lead, ends in Saturn, has to do with the abandonment of understanding. So if you follow those chakras, this one in the forehead opens up, you just see things, and this one at the top of the head receives whatever drops in: Hiya, glad you're here. It has nothing to do with figuring out or feeling through either. Lead is cold and it does not move. I do not know if it is full circle, I think it is a different sort of thing. One is at the beginning and the other is at the end, so there must be some difference.

From early Greek to late Roman times, superstitious curses were inscribed on leaden tablets, and these curses literally meant "bindings." They were left in tombs, buried for the spirits of the underworld. In other words, if you wanted to curse somebody, or bring bad luck to somebody, or get revenge on somebody, you wrote your curse on a leaden tablet and buried it in the tomb of that dead person. In popular imagination, Saturn had a special relationship with spirits beyond the grave and the black art of manipulating those spirits. The idea was that it was not only in people. In the older way of looking at the world, before Descartes, before we divided the world into subjectivity and the object as dead matter out there, everything in the world could be read as belonging to one or another of the gods. Like the cold winter and the bare trees belonged to Saturn, and a hard-shelled nut, the hickory nut, belonged to Saturn. Not a peanut, because that is too easy to crack and open, it is soft. A hickory nut or a walnut, the bones of animals, things that were cold and damp, and animals like goats that do not have a lot of fat on them and that are hardy and live on sparse terrain belong to Saturn. Capricorn in the astrological system is a place where Saturn is at home. All things belonged to one or another of the archetypal principles or gods. So that if you wanted to understand the world, you had to read the world carefully to see what its qualities were. Was it sharp and prickly like a thorn or red pepper? Then it belonged to

Mars. Was it milky and soft? Then it belonged to the Moon. Was it hard and dense and cold? Then it belonged to Saturn. And so you knew what medicines to take, you knew what food to eat, you knew what places to go to. Every place, every province, every river had these qualities. These are the qualities of the world, and you knew where you were all the time. You were under the aegis of one or another of the archetypal principles by the locus, the weather, the food you ate, the wine you drank, the animals you were with, and so on. You were living in a world that was infused with meaning and required careful perception. You had to see and read what was there.

I need to say something about the sexuality of depression. In the melancholic condition there is said to be a giant loss of libido. Impotence goes along with it. There is no interest in sexuality, no active sexual drive. The very word "frigidity," which is such a cruel word used about women, does not actually belong to women. I think it is a Saturnian word projected onto women for that coldness, for impotence and frigidity. What the ancients said about this was that at the same time as there was a decline in actual sexual activity, there was an increase of sexual fantasy. Albertus Magnus says, "The effect of lead is cold and constricting, and it has a special power over sexual lust and nocturnal emissions."[98] So there was the decline of sexual activity and yet an increase of sexual fantasy. That *furor melancholicos,* that creativity that is supposed to go with the melancholic temperament, is also a heightened sexuality of the mind. And we still have that. We have the dirty old man. We have that in the sexual art of old painters. Picasso is the best example. In 1968, in his late eighties, he made 347 pornographic etchings, all in about eight months,[99] and everybody condemned him for being a dirty old man. Why is not what he was doing great art? It was an example of this intense activity of the fantasy life, of the imagination. The Latin term for this is *vis imaginalis,* the force of imagining. Imaginal

98. Albertus Magnus, *Book of Minerals,* translated by Dorothy Wyckoff (Oxford: Clarendon Press, 1967), 210.

99. Published in *Picasso 347,* 2 vols. (New York: Random House/Maecenas Press, 1970).

force increased, owing to Saturn, as the physical force decreased. It is part of a heightened *vis imaginalis,* heightened imaginative force. Therefore, so many of the Renaissance writers and painters considered themselves melancholics, because that was the most vital kind of imagination. Michelangelo lived into his eighties and considered himself a worn out, useless old man. They all refer to themselves already as old when they are in their forties, and some lived into their eighties. Torquato Tasso was another one who had a vivid sexual imagination. Michelangelo's sexual imagination was too much for the church, and later they tried to cover up all kinds of things he had painted in the Sistine Chapel. But its in his later work as well as his writing. He wrote exaggerated love poems when he was quite old. So I think this bears on the clinical work also. When you are working with depressed people, I do not think it is right to just say, well, their libido is gone, that it goes with the depression. It is also good to enquire what sorts of fantasies are going on. Whether they are depressed or whether they are old. It is not to pry, it is not prurience. It is to recognize that there is a vitality inside there. Saturn was the patron god of eunuchs and celibates, that is, those who could not do it. On the other hand, he was also represented by the dog and the goat, both of which were considered to be lecherous creatures. So there you have it: the lechery of the imagination and the impotence of the body.

*The Idea of Treatment*

In order to discuss treatments, we have to expand the notion of treatment so that it is placed within a broad framework rather than simply to say "this is the wound, and this is the bandage," or "this is the fever, and this is the pill." From the alchemical view, depression is an *operation.* It is something that is doing something. It is part of a process and it is doing something. And the terms that apply—mortification, putrefaction, torture—are all parts of the alchemical operation, part of the work of alchemy. So the man, and it was usually men doing the alchemy, the man in the laboratory working on the *materia* is *torturing* it. Jung wrote about this torture.[100] Is it the *materia* that is being tortured? Is it the alchemist being tortured? Who is the torturer? Is it the process itself that is torturing

---

100. See *CW* 13: 139 n. 1.

both of them? What is the torture that goes on in the work of alchemy? One of the main words for this was *mortification*, making things dead, or feeling mortified, shamed, ruined, unable, ground down. The point is that the mortification was very much like the mortar that you put your herbs or spices or seeds in, and then the pestle grinds them down so that they are no longer living seeds but powders. It is a chemical operation. By the reduction to the powder form they can be used and mixed with other things more easily than when they are in seed form. But grinding the seed down is also removing the vitality from it. Now that is like taking the hope out of it. It is removing the vitality from it so that cannot do what it intends to do. By grinding down its natural vital push. That is one of the things depression does. It takes the vitality out of our natural, habitual urging, our forward moving. Another word for this depressive operation in alchemy is *putrefaction*. That is equivalent to the feeling that I am no good, I am rotten, this marriage stinks, my relationships stink, this is all full of shit, all the stuff I am saying, talking about, my relationships. This sense of the putrefying of one's life, the putrefying of one's values, one's heart, one's personality, one's relationships. It is another one of the operations of alchemy that belongs among the depressive part of the work.

So things are killed, blackened, rotted, and cruelly hurt. The mortification, there is cruelty in it. When you grind up your own spices, you have to put a lot of cruelty in it. It is a sadistic operation. You know cooking has lots of sadism in it, if you've ever dismembered or gutted a chicken or pulled its feathers off. You are using big knives and you are chopping. We also peel the skin—we skin things, flame them, break all the eggs.

What I am suggesting, from the alchemical view, is that depression is an *activity*. Something active is happening. You sit there immobilized, but from an alchemical point of view something active is happening. The very fact that it can get you to sit immobilized in a chair is already quite an action in view of the compulsion in the society to keep moving.

Now it is a big moral crisis in life to be able to see how corrupt your life is. What is going on in these darkenings or in this phase in alchemy, are all things that have to do with the *work of the soul*. You begin to see your life is corrupt, or that life in general is corrupt. You get a dark eye for seeing the world. Instead of a naive eye, optimistic, innocent. And probably the more innocent and stupid you are, the more you need to be putrefied and mortified. Because the great universal American sin is

innocence: "I don't know. I'm just a child." The addiction to innocence—
we do not have any recovery groups for that one. We do not even want
to know how many were killed in Iraq. It is not that the government will
not tell us. Nobody wants to know.

In the alchemical model, it is the *nigredo,* the blackening of the work,
wherein things become pulverized, mortified, and putrefied. You have the
feeling that you stink, your marriage stinks, and your life stinks, and it is
all falling apart into pieces that do not fit together. It is all been pulverized,
dried out. This is a state that is necessary for the soul to go through in
the alchemical work, a stage in one's way of thinking. Because what is
coagulated must first be dissolved. That is an alchemical rule. And what
is dissolved must be coagulated. So what is coagulated, what is firm and
solid and in good shape—call it a strong ego—must be dissolved. And
what is chaotic and flowing everywhere needs some kind of coagulation.
And what does that work is this early stage called the *nigredo.* But this
does not just happen in an early stage. It returns again and again in the
work, whenever a new process is to begin. So it is never done and over
with. That is seeing as a *state,* not as a *stage.* It means there is something
of great value in the darkness. The black sun, the raven, the silence, the
fact that you are now in the land of the invisibles. The only way you can
get into the land of the invisibles is to be utterly dark yourself. You learn
of the night, and there is no reason to leave that darkness as a stage to
progress to something better. The jazz musicians stayed in the darkness
and produced everything in the darkness and outside of the mainstream.
You know, you have to realize that there are cultures that have lost their
power in the world and remained in a kind of depressed state for centuries,
like the Portuguese or the Turks. It is a fact that culture does not require
to always win and be on top. The extraordinary culture that has come
from the Black slaves in America that were oppressed, ruined, violated
in every possible way, and all that continuing *after* the great war of liberation of 1861 to 1865, as if the war had never happened until 1965. And
the extraordinary gift to this melting pot that has come from a people
that remained in that *nigredo* state for so long. So, we must not always
think of a *dynamic* process. What do you do with the dark stone? How
do you live with the dark stone? That is the difference between seeing it
as a state or as a stage.

Whereas lead was regarded as a very important and useful metal earlier, before we knew chemically about lead poisoning, lead has curiously become in our society one of the most dangerous things to have around the house. A pinhead of old lead paint on a windowsill is a gigantic hazard for a child. The new statistics on the amount of lead that can be actually ingested are amazing, and it does not go away. It accumulates and eventually results in lowered intelligence, and so on. This is part of the enormous change in our attitude towards lead. In Roman times, all the drinking vessels and plumbing systems were made of lead. Not only in the drinking vessels, it was in the little vessels that used to make *garum*—a fermented fish sauce made with rotten fish and salt. They put it on all kinds of food, and it was kept in these little leaden vessels—like pewter but made with a high lead content. One of the fantasies of the decline of the Roman Empire is that the plumbing and these food vessels produced sterility in the upper classes. The poorer people used clay vessels and so they could propagate, but the upper classes degenerated because of lead poisoning. This is what we think about it now. My point is only that as late as the seventeenth century there were still lead medicines. The alchemists talked of lead poisoning, but they did not mean what is meant by the EPA. They meant that the alchemists get caught by fate, get caught by all kinds of past burdens. I think part of our therapy is lead-poisoned. That it is trapped in the heaviness of the past: karma, fate, childhood, ruins of long ago that weigh on our thinking about the soul. That is like having a lead-poisoned theory. You are imprisoned by what you were, imprisoned by what happened to you, imprisoned by your genetic structure, imprisoned by your parents or absence of parents, by the cruelties of the past. A lot of that is a leaden kind of thinking, and I think you have lead poisoning if you can think only that way.

There was a Saturnian mysticism about the whole alchemical work. Part of it was that there was a depressive view in alchemy, a depressive view of human nature. Owing, maybe, to a Christian overlay. For example, one of the quotes from alchemy is: "Lead signifies the vexations and troubles wherewith God visits us and brings us back to repentance."[101] Now that is a Christian vision of the necessity of repentance, for salvation, and the only way you are going t o repent is if you are somehow forced to it. But

---

101. Vigenerus, "De igne et sale," *Theatr. chem.*, VI, p. 76; quoted in *CW* 14: 472 n. 289.

this is not only Christian. There is even a term, *alchemical melancholy,* that refers to the long sadness in the work. Its the sense you have, when you enter long-term therapy, of being an outcast. The sense, at the beginning of therapy, of being different, isolated, outcast, unable to explain it, on the outside. It used to be that way. Now so many people are in therapy that it is hard to find somebody who is not. But, still, there is the feeling of the lonely wanderer. And there is the language of the journey. This is also a Saturnian fantasy. It is Saturn, the god of the lonely wanderer, he who is in exile, the wandering Jew.

Within the cosmology of alchemy, the treatment is not to get rid of the lead but to understand the lead as performing a function. One of the loveliest of these alchemical ideas that used to be repeated in Persian, Armenian, and Syriac texts—in Middle Eastern alchemy—is that lead makes the diamond suffer; it breaks the diamond.[102] Now you know, and I know, because we are all modern scientific people, that lead is one of the softest of all metals and that the diamond is considered the hardest mineral. So how in the world could lead break a diamond? What is being said with that metaphor, with that little tiny allegory? If you take a steel hammer and try to crack a diamond, you cannot do it. Diamonds are used for polishing steel. So what is being said by "lead makes the diamond suffer; it breaks the diamond?" How would you grapple with that thought? What is this diamond that is broken by lead? Time? Time breaks everything, wears it down. What we value? What we hold to be most valuable? Or what has crystallized as the utterly perfected spiritual quality? You have finally got it all together, and then comes melancholy. You have finally got clarity. You have achieved perfection, whether it is a belief system or some spiritual truth. The diamond body is a big image in Buddhism. Melancholy cracks it. It shows the power, the effectiveness of depression. Now, if it can do all that, from an alchemical point of view, it must be of enormous value. More valuable in a sense than the diamond. This is a crucial insight about the importance of the soul with regard to the spirit. The soul can make the spirit suffer. The spiritual disciplines do their best to keep you cheerful. You may have a dark night of the soul and you may go through hell or something, but the idea is still that melancholy

---

102. Berthold Laufer, *The Diamond: A Study in Chinese and Hellenistic Folklore* (Chicago: Field Museum of Natural History, 1915), 26.

is a no-no. It should be transcended with clarity, purity, truth, spiritual virtues. I believe that melancholy is a soul-making activity that produces depth, inwardness.

Let us go back to that idea of "beginning and ending in lead" that I spoke of a couple of times. What this suggests to me, psychologically, is a sense of time, and the importance of time as an absolute factor in life, in the soul. It suggests the limits of time and the feeling of being limited by time. Realizing that you are limited in time is the root of self-limitation. If you are limited, then you "can't." One of the things that melancholy does for you is to make you feel that: "I can't." Now that is a statement of limits. It pulls in the limits, shrinks them. But also, if we say it begins in lead and ends in lead, then it is also a realization of something else limiting you. It is not just that I am limited, but that the gods limit me. "I can't." "I can't go beyond these limits." And this also gives way to a sense of imagining, because you can imagine beyond the limits. As I said before, the impotence in the body brought on by the lead, senex is paralleled by the *vis imaginalis,* so that, on the one hand, the old man can't—there is this impotence—and on the other hand, he can much more than anyone else in his fantasies. It limits release or invites the extension of imagination. Goethe is supposed to have said that one day in the world would be enough for him to spend the rest of his life in a cell remembering and imagining all that was given to him in that one day.

I think another important aspect of the beginning and ending in lead is that at the beginning the feeling of being odd, dysfunctional, neurotic, leads to a sense of exile, a sense that that one is fundamentally in exile and therefore related to invisible powers. But at the beginning, you only feel the exile. At the end of the work, you still feel the exile, but the exile is not an exile from you and me in relationship, but an exile from the world of the dead, of the ancestors, of the spirits—the invisibles. That is the big exile, and that is another problem of therapy again. Therapy, as a secular activity, does not understand exile in the larger sense. It does not understand loneliness in terms of exile, and so it sees loneliness in terms of relationship. You follow me there? Loneliness in terms of relationship means you are constantly working on relationship in order to get your soul right. Relationship with the therapist, relationship of transference, etc. until you are sick with it and never realizing that the exiled condition, that tradition after tradition talks about—Jewish, Christian, Persian, Sufi, and so on—means that the return to the other world is the crucial part. You do not build your soul's satisfaction on the relationship to a significant other in this world. That is a very important theme in Sufism for example, in all those translations of Rumi's poems by Coleman Barks, there is a whole big theme of separation.[103]

Now in alchemical thinking, in pre-element thinking, lead contains iron, tin, and copper. So one would have to imagine what the iron is in the lead. Is that what is meant when we say that depression is masked anger? That there is iron, the element of Mars, in the lead, that is, the element of weapons, the element of the iron age, of the industrial age. And when they say there is copper in the lead, is there a feeling of Venus in lead? Is there a beauty in the lead. Is there a sweetness, a softness, a sensitivity, a receptivity, a connection? When they disintegrate the lead into these three components, they are saying there is knowledge in the depression that is withheld, and the knowledge would be copper, tin, and iron. Tin is the metal of Jupiter, and that suggests there is a kind of capacity to imagine in great extension, as Zeus does. It is Jupiter/Zeus who can imagine all the forms of the world. He was king of the gods. So within his imaginative capacity were all the other capacities. He could imagine beyond any of the others, and that is this expansiveness of tin. Tin can be hammered into all kinds of reflective and large and strange shapes. I am doing all this pretty fast. I am doing this in order to give a background to the sense of treatment, because as long as treatment is seen as a surgical treatment, as an exorcism, or as long as treatment is seen as a cure, you are not valuing the thing as it is. You are not valuing the fact that there may be an intention in it. The alchemists would not treat it. They would try to refine it, bring out the other things latent in it, find the secret knowledge that is hidden within, or respect the destruction that is going on with it as within a larger process of soul-making. So the idea of treatment within an alchemical model suggests a recognition of virtues within. I am trying to extend the notion of treatment.

---

103. See also Fariba Mansouri, "Longing for Belonging: Exile and Homecoming in Rumi's Poetry and Jung's Psychology," PhD diss., Pacifica Graduate Institute, 2010.

It is hard for me to shift to talking about what we have come to mean by treatment today. So maybe, instead, I will just continue talking about this other meaning of treatment, about treatment by means of the gods. Now another aspect of the alchemical model is that the things under pressure can change. That is, things within the vessel are subjected to intensity of heat, passion, and attention. Attention produces heat, if you just keep looking at something, just keep focused on it (the word *focus* in Latin means hearth, oven). So focus is a heat-making activity, and if you just keep focused, then things change. That is a basic idea of alchemy. The change that the blackening, the *nigredo,* the darkness undergoes, is first of all to become more black than it was to begin with. The work does not begin until the black has become black all the way through. It has to be blacker than black, suggesting that it has to be unimaginably black, not even literally black, but completely blackened, burnt out totally, impossible, nothing left, not even ash. I do not know how else to describe it. It is a complete negativity, blacker than black, blacker than a raven's wing. Now this is one model against which you can place those feelings that go on in depression. It does not let up, it just gets worse. There is no light at the end of the tunnel, there is just another tunnel. I actually had a dream like that years ago. I thought I had come through something or other, and when I got to where it was to end, it turned out you were supposed to go back, but at another, deeper level! I remember another person's dream where they were in a swimming pool and had to swim under water for I do not know how long, and when they got to the end, they do not come up for air but turn around and swim back. The repetition is a very important part of this melancholic experience. The return of the symptoms, the return of the repressed, the fact that it keeps coming back when you think you are done with it. See, you can never decide when you are done with it. It somehow decides when its done with you! That assumes intention in it. It does not leave you until it is done with you, or it is done to you what it wants to do. You see the way I am talking is attempting to place the intentionality outside of the ego, outside of the subject, so that the victimization takes on a new quality. The victim, after all, is that which is sacrificed at an altar. It is a tribute to a god, an offering. As long as you keep the victim held inside the ego you can never be released from victimization. It is simply an insult and an outrage. So what it is intending, in the alchemical vision of this kind of suffering, what it is intending is for the black eventually to turn white. The transition from the black to white is via the *blue*, in the way I have set it up, and I find a lot of evidence for that. You must understand that everybody talks alchemy in his or her own way. There is no unified system of alchemy, there are just endless numbers of texts, and everybody interprets them according to the things they want to use alchemy for. I am following Jung here in that tradition of using alchemy to draw psychological insights.

The blue comes when the black breaks into song, when you can begin to lament. Because when it is in the black, you have no voice even to speak of what is happening. It is silent. But when it begins to turn blue, words can come out: lamentation, complaints, all the blues songs: "She done me wrong, and now she is gone." And that blueing is the beginning of a kind of imagination of the black, a verbalization, symbolization, connecting it to something beyond, less literal, less condensed, or less dense, opening out into the blue, or opening down into the deep blue. Therefore, people are right when they are afraid that when you have got the blues, you may sink into a morbid depression, because the blue and the black are very close. I do not know if one can give a therapeutic dose of blue. Can you dose yourself with inoculations of blue so that you do not get the big blackness? I do not know. A certain amount of blue time, a certain amount of down time so that it does not hit all at once? I do not know.

I think that longing, the blues, would be part of what the ancient alchemy of the Egyptians meant when it said there is copper in the lead. That is the Venusian or erotic element, the love element, the yearning for love, the *pothos* as I have called it.[104]

We should now speak about the treatments of Venus rather than Saturn. The Venusian treatments, which maybe for milder depression, were laid out mainly in the Renaissance where diet was extremely important. What

---

104. "Pothos: The Nostalgia of the Puer Eternus," in James Hillman, *Loose Ends: Primary Papers in Archetypal Psychology* (Thompson, Conn.: Spring Publications, 2022 [1975]).

one was to eat was fresh eggs, young meat like veal, salads, fruit, especially grapes, all food with a lot of liquid and moisture. A light diet. It is interesting that we start the day in America often not only with coffee but with orange juice. The color of orange is the great extravert flaming, martial, brightening stuff that you wake up with, and then the coffee, and maybe some sugar. Now that gets you launched into the manic day! The Scotts begin with oatmeal or maybe haggis, which is a sheep's stomach, limed and boiled. That is hardly optimistic is it?! But it goes with the bagpipes.

The Venusian treatment also consists of moistening the air and sweetening the air. And we do, we take flowers to people in the hospital, the sick room, a curious habit that is unreflected but that is bringing Venus into the sick room. What kind of flowers is not the important thing. It is driving the bad spirit out of the room and bringing another kind of spirit into the room, assuming that these flowers have a spirit in them. They believed in baths, lots of different kinds of baths with red, yellow, green, and white additives. In other words, The Body Shop. The Body Shop all through America is an anti-depressive place where you can get the bright colored liquids, smells, and ointments to soften, sweeten, and lighten the day. This is a kind of Venusian treatment. I think we get that all the time, the Venusian spa treatment. Just think about how good it is to take a bath. Not a shower. How good it is to take a bath, and how good it is to get massaged and have oil put on your body, and how much time is spent with cosmetics. We incorporate these Venusian treatments unconsciously into our lives to feel better. I think most people have found a way to make their slight moments of depression livable through these Venusian modes, like going to a spa or taking a bubble bath.

Sweetening the air was based on the important idea that Saturn produced bad airs or that melancholy hangs on to thick, dark, bad smelling air. It *likes* that kind of atmosphere. There is the idea that certain things *like* other things. An apricot tree likes the morning sun, so you plant it there. Roses like dry and a lot of heat. Melancholy likes thick, bad-smelling air. The depressive person loves to remain in foul, putrid, closed-in air. If you've ever visited your relatives who are depressed, who are old, with what is called involutional melancholy, they do not want to get out, they do not want new furniture, they do not want new dresses, they do not want new clothes, they do not want to change their clothes, they do not want to bathe. They just want to sit there, and the air gets fetid, the psychic air gets fetid. That is why Saturn is the god of privies, of toilets, and dirty linen. He likes that atmosphere. You sweeten the air in order to drive away or make it inhospitable for Saturn or for melancholy. You may carry with you a sweet potion, some sweet smelling ointment. Not some smelling salts to shock you awake, but something to keep the airs around you sweet and light, like perfume or aftershave—to keep depression away. There was a fastidious focus on remedies, and these remedies were of all sorts. You could read about these remedies in Burton's *The Anatomy of Melancholy*. He devotes whole chapters to the various elixirs, pills, balms, and the kind of sleeping equipment you should have and what you should have under your pillow, and what kind of pillow, and which bands you would wear on your forehead to keep your thoughts from being oppressed by Saturn, which could be dipped in different liquids so that they would have a fragrance—mint, for instance, or whatever was good for lightening the air and lightening the mood. How far away this kind of thinking is from treatment as we think of it now! And how unpleasant the rooms generally are where people suffer from their melancholy.

The question of the chronic and the acute is very important because some of the most devastating treatments ever in psychiatry have been invented for dealing with depression. There is something in the medical model of thinking that goes all the way back to Apollo. One of his epithets was *He hastens to help.* That hastening is crucial for emergency, for the battlefield surgeon, for the accident, the crisis. But it is an *acute* thinking. Because depression is not acute, there is a terrible frustration in the person dealing with it, and so extraordinary measures have been invented to deal with it, electroshock only being the last in a long list of violent therapies. There were sorts of cruel methods that were usually employed with depressives, such as the dunking stool in the early 1800s where a patient was put into a chair and was dunked in and out of cold water. Or the use of hoses on naked patients in the asylums to stimulate them, wake them up, like fire hoses. Or the tranquilizer stool or chair. It was called a tranquilizer chair. You sat in, and it spun you around until you were dizzy, and that was supposed to rearrange your mental order. And there was the forced feeding, metal contraptions that were put into the mouth to hold the jaw open so that food could be forced down your gullet like a goose producing *fois gras*. Some of the major physical treatments used in this century were all invented in the middle of the 1930s in countries like Portugal, Hungary, and Italy, that were then under Fascist regimes. I am talking about insulin shock, and electric shock, which was invented by Ugo Cerletti in Italy in 1938. He was an electro-specialist who invented the delayed fuses on the shells of anti-aircraft guns. The shell was fired into the air but did not explode until it reached a certain altitude, and therefore it required a delayed fuse. He invented that too. In his journals it says he had observed in slaughter houses that hogs that had been given an electric shock through the temples did not resist having their throats slit. Cerletti's first human victim was a vagrant, that is an old word for the homeless, arrested for riding a train without a ticket. After the first 80-volt shock, the vagrant who had been up to that time incoherent, said clearly, "Not another one, it is deadly." Although Cerletti's colleagues urged him to discontinue the experiment, he ignored them, applying thirteen treatments in all to the original victim, some at even higher voltages.

Now the psychiatric text books say there is hardly been a treatment more effective than electroconvulsive therapy (ECT). It is an extremely effective treatment, and it works very quickly. People are no longer in those extraordinarily deep depressions after it. The anti-psychiatry people say electroshock therapy's popularity may be due in part to the fact that it is extremely lucrative.

These radical and violent methods of treatment reflect the anger and frustration in the therapist against this obdurate depression that does not move. You will find it in yourself working with depressive people. I have some friends who already are therapists who find that. I am thinking of a psychiatrist in particular who will not work with depressives. He gets too angry. Think about that. It sets off a very acute reaction. A German psychiatrist, H.-J. Wilke,[105] a Jungian, has written a small and very useful paper saying that there is no patient that brings out more hostility in the therapist than the depressive. He pointed out how the attempt to attack

---

105. H.-J. Wilke, "On Depressive Delusion," *Spring: A Journal of Archetype and Culture* (1978): 105–14.

the depression produces a split archetype. You get an angry therapist and a depressed, laconic, immobile patient. The depression releases a huge amount of rage and cruelty in the therapist. Now it is not just a martial cruelty, because Saturn is also the god of cruelty, and so it is almost treating like with like. The sadistic aspect of the therapy. You hate your patients! That is part of the problem. You hate them because nothing is happening, nothing is moving. They do not give any answers, they just sits there, and get dirtier and messier, and dumber and quieter, and all of that fury builds up because you come out of an acute fantasy. So the chronic way of working is accompaniment: walking along together or sitting still together. And all sense of going somewhere or getting somewhere, there is no arrow of time any longer. You know that Peter Sellers movie, *Being There*? It is just being there. And watching what is there, carefully. That sense of craft. And then Wilke says something important. He reminds us of Freud, that in the depressive delusion important things are going on. Freud said, "He must in some way be right," meaning the patient, "and he must be describing something that actually is and as he imagines it to be."[106] Freud is giving complete authority to the delusion the patient is suffering. "He must be in some way right, and he must be describing something that is and as he imagines it to be." And Wilke turns that to say, "The patient is making serious statements about hidden reality." So I am reminding you that a depressive patient evokes sadism somewhere or another—either the patient is punishing himself sadistically, or he catches you in a sadistic fantasy. And what we do to our own depressions is often sadistic too. We have no time for it. We are cruel to it. We give it no comfort.

In regard to electroshock, psychiatry generally said, and still says, that the effect of ECT in depression is one of the most spectacular treatments in medicine. Now whether they mean spectacular in the visible sense of what you are seeing or whether they mean spectacular in the effects I do not know. I think they mean the latter. However, let us also remember that they also say, "We are very successfully treating conditions of unknown cause with treatments of an equally unknown mode of action." Now that is not surprising because what the history of medicine shows is that

---

106. In his essay "Mourning and Melancholia" (1917).

what matters in pragmatic medicine, which developed particularly in the eighteenth century, is not the cause and how to deal with the cause, but what medicine actually works. How it works is a great mystery. But what works? ECT works. We do not know how it works, but it works. Let us leave out the side effects. I do not know enough about them. There are all kinds of reports of side effects.

I do not know when to prescribe it or to whom to prescribe it. I only know that the idea of shocking a patient out of a severe depression—a shocking—is a very old idea. You bring a quick insight to someone, and it is a shock to get that realization. The idea is that a shock rearranges your psychic structure. It can be concretized into electricity, but it can also be psychological shock. If there is ECT, then it is your job as a psychotherapist to continue your relation to the psyche, all the time. I am trying to get us freed, as psychotherapists, from *overvaluing* the physical methods of treatment, because the moment you overvalue them, you are fallen into your medical shadow, and you are more interested in dosage and arguing about medicine and all the rest of it than treating the soul of the patient. And as I have said all along, *the psyche is always present.* There is always something psychological to do—always. Even if the person is incarcerated, even if the person is strapped into a straitjacket, there is still a human being that your psyche can be with. And our lack of insight into our own medical shadow catches us enormously so that our first question is often, What are you taking for it? We are part of a medicalized world in which we all think so medically. We think, How did I get it? Oh, there was the woman behind me who coughed on the train, or it was the kid who came home from school with a runny nose. We think about contagion, we think medically, and yet we practice psychology. We have to learn a lot about freeing ourselves from being trapped in the medical model. John Layard, who I mentioned before and who said "depression is withheld knowledge," he had been in, I do not know how many, different kinds of therapy when he was younger. He went to see a famous English therapist in the 1930s, and he was in such bad shape that he arrived in a taxi lying on the floor of the cab. He was unable to look out the windows, unable to sit up. And he went in to see the therapist, and he began by telling him the medications that he was on, and the man said to him, You know, take whatever you want. I mean, whatever you are taking, you take, that is not what we are going to be doing here. He completely dismissed the medications. Made it entirely secondary. And constellated him in his psychological mode, focused on what we are going to be doing here, talking or whatever else they did. He always told me that story as illustrating a genius stroke dismissing the power of the magic of the pills. Because the patient was hung up on what he was taking, whether he should be taking, what are the effects, watching himself whether it was putting him to sleep or whether it was not. He was becoming like a laboratory rat. I mean, that can be bio-feedback information, but at the same time he was losing his psychological concerns.

Now another treatment is purging. This is a big one. This is probably as violent as the electroshock. Because you were imagined to have a surface of black bile in your body—*melancholia*—you were internally being poisoned, and that poison was in turn giving you the disease called depression or melancholy. Therefore, the job was to purge it. The best way to purge it was to use violent purgatives, mainly one made with hellebore, a herb that produces violent bowl movements It is so violent that it often caused internal bleeding. Internal bleeding produces a black stool, so part of the evidence of the success of the cure was *shitting black*. Perfectly rational medical thinking. Besides, bleeding people was not thought to be so bad. Anal bleeding was a major therapy for depression. One part of this is that it released this bitter mood that was concretized into the black bile. This bitterness, this hatred, was blown out through the anus. Now if you think about this in terms of Freud and the anal character, they've really got something. They are talking about opening the anal sphincter, releasing that tightness, that Saturnian control, that tight, bitter, holding-on aspect of Saturn, by blowing it out the anus. Now people still have this fantasy today. There are plenty of ads in the newspaper for high colonics with lovely little pictures of your large intestine all crinkly. You have probably seen them. If you read the *LA Weekly*, you can see one each week. You start with the crinkly areas, and then when it is all blown out with a high colonic enema, it becomes all nice, smooth, clean, and happy. And lots of people go through these cures. They go regularly to get themselves cleaned out. Getting rid of that "bad" stuff that is in there. And that bad stuff is a Saturnian idea. It is the bad stuff. It smells bad, which is bad air. Remember, Saturn is the god of outhouses, dirty linen, bad smells, isolation. So you are getting Saturn out of your system with the high colonic, and the imagination is in the realm of fecal fantasies. As I said before, one of the effects of depression is in constipation. So you are changing the situation by working on that particular area and that particular symptom.

I think this has a lot of violence in it, a lot of aggression. The idea was to purge out the system by bleeding, by salts, or by enemas—by radical catharsis. These purges were violent. Hellebore produces cramps, spasms, and violent diarrhea. The point that they were making was they were getting rid of the cause of melancholia. Now this idea of a radical attack on the disease is still part of the shock treatment. And maybe there are ways of psychologically radically shocking the patient. Direct aggressive attack, confrontation, accusation that the patient is simply using the depression in order to manipulate his wife, that he is so fucked up in his mother complex that all he can do is complain. Radical aggressive interpretation. He smells. Have you ever told a patient that he smells? That his body smells? That he or she has not washed? This notion of shock, of radical purging, is trying to drive out the demon of depression, the complex that has got this person into an identity with it. And it is possible, it is possible *if* that is your style and you know how to do it. An aggressive attack on the *complex*, not on the person, may be very valuable.

You know, the question of violence is a difficult thing because we do not have, except for football, much ritualized violence. We do not have possibilities of joining groups and formalizing the urge for violence, so it gets randomized. We still worship the random, free individual not caught in any ceremonies. And so a consequence of that freedom is that we worship random violence rather than ritual violence. Two places that deal with violence the most, the military and the gangs, are both hierarchically organized in ritual form. Sports, too, but there is a kind of political correctness that is crept into sports where a guy that is made a touchdown can no longer do his little sexy dance or spike the ball. Certain things that go with the exuberance, that are part of the dance of the ritual—we have cleaned that stuff up.

*Other Imaginings of Treatment*

Now there are other cures that are not quite as violent. If we use homeopathy as the lead cure, not in the way I have described it earlier, but homeopathically, you would cure lead with lead. Now what would that be? Homeopathically and psychologically, it would be a deepening. Not finding out the causes of my life, but archeological fantasies, digging deep into history. Deep solitude, deep numbers, mathematics, geometry, abstractions. Deep study. Not digging only into the past of oneself, but digging in another way. In the eighteenth century, that idea of digging into archeology was actually one of the treatments for depression. Let me tell you a little bit about that now. In eighteenth-century in England, the disease was called the English malady, sometimes called spleen, and sometimes hypochondria. It, of course, affected the upper class. Today we would call it neurosis or neurasthenia, but maybe we would not be allowed to use those words anymore because they are eliminated from the DSM. I do not know what we would call them, suffering from narcissistic borderline panic attacks or something or other. These people were malingers—that is, they were always ill and unable to get it together. They were depressed, and the climate oppressed them. Now this class of people had private physicians or companions who took them on trips to the classical world. And they went on the Grand Tour of Italy in order to look at the ruins and the great art. And this was a distinct treatment for the English malady. The symptoms of the English malady were sweating, sickness, depression, suicide, masturbation, and vapors. Boswell, Stern, Walpole, Goldsmith all made the trip to Italy. Now think about it. Think about this mode of treatment. First of all, they were not looking at themselves. They were looking at images. They were not looking at their own personal ruin but at ancient ruins, magnificent ruins, the ruin exaggerated and busted in such a way that fantasy could fill out the ruin. It stimulated them. You know, going to the ruins always stimulates fantasy because you fill out the missing pieces like a gestalt or a TAT test.[107] Your mind begins to imagine. So what they were doing in this cure was feeding the imagination. It is the major way I see treatment. They saw great art works, paintings, statues. They saw the gods, polytheism. They got out of England and saw the Mediterranean. They were put back in touch with something other than the dismal Church of England. They were moving not in the way you move during exercise but moving through geography, through

---

107. Thematic Apperception Test. Popularly known as the "picture interpretation technique," it was developed by American psychologists Henry A. Murray and Christina D. Morgan at Harvard University in the 1930s.

landscape. And I see this as a Jupiterian kind of treatment, an expansion. An expansion of imagination.

The Grand Tour of the young wealthy English in the 1700s, which took them through beautiful Italian landscapes, was not just a pleasure trip. It was, of course, also about young men being able to learn about the world. But, at the same time, it was a way of mollifying melancholy. The melancholy was so strong because of the climate, the darkness, and the discipline of the schools, so the trip to Italy was a chance to expand the soul of the melancholic young person. It was not merely a culture trip. Now if we could think about that a little bit more, we might be able to invent modes of working the imagination of the depressive so that he or she becomes melancholic. That is what I have been saying all along: to move it into a Romantic fantasy. The sources of the Romanticism are the Italian Greek fantasies of the gods and goddesses. That is all of what is in Shelley, Byron, and the early German Romantics. I think this way of looking at things is quite extraordinary. They did not say that the trips healed or cured the melancholy, but many of them found that it was a way of convalescence, a way of softening its hardships.

Another treatment recommended in that time was again going back to the moistening, to the eighteenth century and even earlier: the baths. The natural springs that had warm water baths were used by people all over Europe. American Indians also used warm water baths. I do not know what for, I am not awake enough in that culture to know. The idea of moistening the soul seems to me a very important idea to help the depressed part of life. We set the day up for our manic life with a brisk shower in the morning. By starting the day off with a slow bath and a bowl of oatmeal, you start the day in another way. These habits are cultural, they are automatic, part of the way we live. Think of the kind of advertisement for the breakfast cereals—pop, crackle, and snap. Crispy, crunchy Cheerios! It suggests that the whole nation needs to be shaken out of a depression to get going.

I have not mentioned music yet. The playing of music to soften the melancholy spirit is found already in King Saul.[108] Because music was thought to have a therapeutic effect, the king summoned a harp player

---

108. 1 Samuel 16:14–23.

named David—because Saul was, as you know, a mad king. And this goes on for a long, long time, the listening to deeper and deeper music, knowing the importance of music. There is a brief passage in Hesiod's *Theogony*:

> For although a man has sorrow and grief in his newly-troubled soul and lives in dread because his heart is distressed, yet, when a singer, the servant of the Muses, chants the glorious deeds of men of old and the blessed gods who inhabit Olympus, at once he forgets his heaviness and remembers not his sorrows at all.
>
> (trans. Hugh G. Evelyn-White)

Singing the songs of the gods. In other words, poetry. There were seven tones of music, and the deepest tone was the Saturnian chord, which would accord with the soul of the depressive person listening, and that would have a soothing effect. Again, the intention is to feed the soul with something. And you realize we do not have much stuff to feed the soul with when we treat people. What do we give them? We are taught to refer them to someone who can prescribe medication, and then what is given to the patient is a dosage, four times a day. If it is a little too much or too little, come back in a week, and maybe you will get a little less or a little more. All these treatments are *giving something*. They are giving baths, they are giving perfumes, they are giving smells, they are giving images, they are giving travel, they are giving music. That, it seems to me, is what archetypal psychology's job is: to find what to give to the patient's soul. That is not exploring the patient, that is not investigating, that is not asking the patient to produce dreams, images, fantasies, memories. Do you realize what we do all the time? We are asking the patient to do that—we do not *give* back, we do not start off by giving.

The Italian Renaissance author, courtier, and diplomat Baldassare Castiglione, one of the masters of education of his time, denied that music, as was thought then, was appropriate only for women.[109] He said music was also appropriate for men. For him, the world is composed of music. The heavens make harmony in their moving, and the soul, being ordered in like fashion, awakens, as it were, and revives its powers through music. The soul revives its powers through music. So it was both the

---

109. Baldesar Castiglione, *The Book of the Courtier*, translated by Charles S. Singleton (Garden City: Anchor Books/Doubleday, 1959 [1528]).

way into death. Music is the bridge to the other world. And if one of the fantasies of depression is suicide—to leave this world for another world or at least to leave this world—then that entrance to the other world can be provided by music.

Now I bet you, those of you who go to regular seminars—keeping your license up to date—you will be taught a lot about the new dosages and new drugs. And probably that whole little convention that you go to has been paid for by Bristol Myers Squibb. But what I am suggesting here is that there is a great deal to learn about treatment. About what to give and dosages that are not literalized and pharmacological. Which is not to say that you cannot use Prozac or Halcion, or whatever else. I am not against them. I am trying to say there is *more* to give a patient than that. There are other cures, other treatments, other modes of working.

### Depression and Political Dysfunction

If we are dysfunctional as citizens, we may be suffering enormously without knowing it. Aristotle said that man is by nature a political animal. Now that is a basic definition of the human being. As a political animal we are, in our guts, in our instincts, in our animal life *political*, members of community. We are instinctually political, members of the *polis*. If you are not living the instinct of politics, could you not be dysfunctional? Could you not be suffering from dysfunctional political instinct as you are suffering from dysfunctional sexual or eating instincts or any other instinct? If that is the case and you are not standing for those instincts but living in a suppressed way, you are a dysfunctional citizen and psychology is not helping you. Because psychology tends to internalize the outrage over some event that occurred during the day. But we are all citizens first and patients second. If you begin to regard the person who comes into your consulting room first of all as a citizen, you are going to talk differently than if you talk to them as a patient. It could be an item in the news, something about banking or corruption, or the school system or something, that is absolutely outrageous to you. And instead of being involved in that emotion, it is internalized and interpreted as your aggression problem, your hostility problem, and so on. That is an internalization of outrage into rage, or into hostility.

The same thing goes on with other emotions like fear. Fear is an informative emotion in relation to the world around you. If you were not afraid, you could not drive your car or walk down the street. You would walk right into the traffic. You must have fear. It informs you about something out there—it is related. Now, on the other hand, anxiety has no object. That is parts of its definition in emotion theory. In emotion theory, the difference is that fear has an object and anxiety is objectless. So what happens? What we have done in therapy, we have taken fear, which is a very important emotion of relatedness, and we talk about a person's anxiety, and anxiety states. And what is feared is called phobic. Buddha says that the whole world is in fear, hence the gesture: fear not. We have to return the emotions to their natural states. And stop them from being interpreted as internal states—fear turned into anxiety, outrage translated into hostility, sadness and mourning translated into depression.

This internalization has made psychotherapy a field where you can work on those internalized emotions, but it has also left the world deprived of those direct emotional reactions. If you see something that makes you sad, images of dead children, that is not because you are depressed. Those images are not depressive, those are sad images and your psyche may want to mourn over that or grieve over that.

*One* aspect of depression may be the fact that you are not living in community, so you are not gaining anything or exchanging with others. You are not living as a citizen. Before that person is a client or a patient, he or she is a citizen. Which would suggest to those of you who are therapists, that when you ask your patients questions in taking a case history, have you ever asked a patient who they voted for? Whether they voted? What party their father belonged to? Anything at all about their political life? We will ask about the whole history of their sexual life, all about their feeling life, but what about their political life? What about the betrayals they may have committed politically? What about the cowardice of their life politically? What about the ducking out? The tremendous political sins we carry within us! Are they brought in to therapy? Therapy is not supposed to be political, it is supposed to be impartial. But if man is by nature a political animal—and Aristotle's definition has endured for a very long time—then we have to recognize this fundamental nature of the human being. You may be sick, dysfunctional, because you are not living your political life.

What I would like you to do is entertain the idea and let it ricochet around awhile rather than immediately concretizing it into a solution. How is this person not political? How are you not political? What is going on there? Or what about music, or the other things I mentioned? Anybody who is totally depressed and lying in bed is not going to do any of these things. But your *imagination* can be working on these things nonetheless. What I am trying to say here is, before you put something into concrete action, entertain it in your mind. Let the idea play around in your mind before you take an idea and apply it. Now that is difficult for us to do because that is not American—it is un-American to do that. Our job is to get an idea and apply it! We think something is a good idea because it works! But in between is a lot of imagination, thought, reflection, speculation, enjoyment, talk, working. That area is what I would like us to be dealing with before *rushing* into application. We get *rid* of ideas by applying them! So we do not have enough ideas!

*The Politics of Depression*

This is sort of a Mort Sahl interlude. I want to talk about the politics. The position I have been holding is that in a manic society, depression is going to be anti-social. It is going against the collective stream, and therefore the treatments for it will also have a societal and political aspect.

We have moved now to a point where the control of the citizen is much less visible than it once was. We are much closer to the kind of world that George Orwell described or the kind of world that is in *Fahrenheit 451*, where Julie Christie is on pills all day long and watching TV, and where book burning, not book saving, is the job of the fire department. It is an extraordinary movie, still very worthwhile seeing.[110] We are in a place now where we think that if we recycle six aluminum cans every day, or if we vote, we have done our citizen's duty, instead of realizing that these are compromise formations of denial and that there is much more to do than recycling or voting. These are points made very strongly by Michael Ventura in his articles.[111] Voting is not enough. And even then, only thirty-

110. *Fahrenheit 451* (1966), directed by François Truffaut, was based on Ray Bradbury's 1953 dystopian novel.

111. Michael Ventura, *Letters at 3 am: Reports on Endarkenment* (Thompson, Conn.: Spring Publications, 2024 [1993].

five percent of the people vote. Most of those who are oppressed by the system do not vote. And when they do vote, well, we have a society where the slaves vote for their masters rather than rebelling against them. The control of the citizen has moved from straitjackets to drugs, from physical measures to pharmacological measures. The great freedom that we felt in opening up the asylums and using pharmacology to deal with the mental outcasts rather than locking them up was, of course, a very big step in freeing people. But in America, because of our dedication to innocence, we always lose the shadow of everything we talk about. So the shadow of freeing the individuals from the asylums was to chain them in a new way, so that we do not think of them in the same way any more. Remember that we talked about the spectrum of depression, from the extreme cases to the cases of normal mourning and grief. What do we want to call these? *Normal* or *usual* depression? But, you see, we are taking a way of thinking about the sickest and applying it to the least sick. That is the danger now. And there has been an extraordinary consciousness of depression in the last few years. There are advertisements in the newspapers about uncovering depression—Depression Awareness, Depression Recognition. And from the National Institute of Mental Health we have Helpful Facts about Depressive Illnesses. Now you see, the more we all become conscious of our depressions, the more we think of ourselves as sick, the more it is necessary to get mental health. And mental health today is largely equated with pharmacology. And as Peter Kramer in his Prozac book[112] pointed out, thirty years ago Valium was the drug of choice. It was to keep women happy and quiet at home. Now Prozac is the drug of choice because it gets them out dating and serving the society. In other words, Prozac belongs to the feminist drug spectrum, and Valium belongs to the patriarchal drug spectrum. I mean these are the ways it is argued about politically. And there is a lot to think about there. There are ads in the newspaper about getting yourself tested to find out if you are depressed or not, because you may not know you that are depressed. The idea is that you do not know that you are sick, but that you can go find out if you have it. Well, it is like TB. You may not know you have TB, so you go and get yourself X-rayed. You may not know you have

---

112. Peter D. Kramer, *Listening to Prozac* (New York: Viking, 1993).

breast cancer, so you get yourself a mammogram. You may not know you are depressed. You fill out the forms, you answer the questionnaire, and you find out that you *are* depressed—and it is a *treatable* illness, just as alcohol is now a disease. Someone's written a book called *Diseasing of America*,[113] and even Illich has worked this over himself in one of his radical and marvelous books.[114] So what I am saying is that there is an entire spectrum of people thinking this way. It is not something original or radical or peculiar to me.

Look at this pamphlet from the National Institute of Mental Health. It explains this public program, a campaign of public education with a motto. You know, like we have Operation Desert Storm, this has a motto too: "Depression: Define it. Defeat it." And it was *launched.* The campaign was launched in 1988. "Depression is a national economic issue." Which means depressives do not shop! Production is no longer *the* issue. Productivity is *an* issue, but consumption is the *real* issue. "Depression is a treatable illness." And there are campaign materials that are produced in English and Spanish, fact sheets, fliers, brochures for the general public, media materials such as print ads, and television and radio public service announcements, etc. Now part of the point here is to improve productivity, reduce time lost from work. Now this is one we should think about too—reduce time lost from work. What happens during that time lost from work? You might be at home, you might do childcare... Think of this in terms of George Orwell. And then, "Avoid costs of prolonged treatment or expensive hospitalization." That implies that there are *quick* ways of dealing with depression, that are not prolonged. In other words, treat it in an acute way. But depression belongs to Saturn. It is a chronic disorder. It takes time. What it requires is time, but here there is a confusion between chronic and acute. "How you can help. Help a depressed person get treatment." Now that goes back to early Christianism where missionary activity and conversion is absolutely essential. You *help* somebody else get into the church. And here it says that there are professional training

---

113. Stanton Peele, *Diseasing of America: Addiction Treatment Out of Control* (Lexington, Mass. and Toronto: Lexington Books/D.C. Heath and Company, 1989).

114. Ivan Illich, *Limits to Medicine. Medical Nemesis: The Expropriation of Health* (London: Marion Boyars, 1976)

programs initiated in 1986. And then the development of television satellite network courses—so that the consciousness of depression is raised in the country. Now there is no doubt that depression is responsible, to use the usual word, for absenteeism, and sexual harassment supposedly, and slowdowns. What are some of the other productive failures? Changing jobs a lot, being dissatisfied and going to work somewhere else, not being able to keep up with the production line schedule. Depression interferes with these. Increasing productivity is the major measure of whether we are keeping up competitively with other nations. Depression becomes an enemy of the state. It is an enemy of productivity. Productivity is tied in with the corporate mind and with the welfare of the nation as an economic power. Depression then becomes the enemy. Those of you old enough will remember in the early 1960s, when Kennedy was president, the enemy was mental retardation, because Kennedy had a sister who was mentally retarded, and there was enormous energy and research in the National Institute of Mental Health on retardation. Then there was a great attack on schizophrenia. You may remember Robert Galbraith Heath at Tulane University injecting spiders with a serum protein fraction of the blood of individuals with a clinical diagnosis of schizophrenia to produced crazy spider webs.[115] I met him actually, and this was considered a breakthrough in schizophrenia research. An enormous amount of National Institute of Mental Health money was spent on schizophrenia research. It was the enemy then. There were so many people suffering from schizophrenia, it was said then. And there were countermovements and countertherapies, for example, John Perry in San Francisco with his clinics in the Haight-Ashbury years showing that schizophrenia had deep meanings and was very important.[116] He had a completely different take. But that was the stuff of the age—Rosen's treatments of schizophrenics by lying down with

---

115. There was speculation that the serum Heath called "taraxein" might be the metabolic toxin X postulated by Jung as the biochemical cause of dementia praecox or schizophrenia (cf. CW 3: 196). Ultimately, the success rate of the taraxein studies declined over time, and its validity was called into question; see M. L. Throne and C. W. Gowdey, "A Critical Review of Endogenous Psychotoxins as a Cause of Schizophrenia," Canadian Psychiatric Association Journal 12, no. 2 (April 1967).

116. John Weir Perry, The Far Side of Madness (Thompson, Conn.: Spring Publications, 2020 [1974].

them feeding them, making love to them, anything at all to interact with them—there were radical therapies, but it was focused on schizophrenia, like it was earlier focused on mental retardation.[117] A little later, we had a lot of attention on childhood syndromes, autism for example. Today, it seems there is a sudden major interest in depression.

So it is a political question. What is in the air of our body politic? How does it connect with a state that is, at the same time, increasing its police force and its prisons and attempting to privatize major public services such as the post office. How do these things belong together? We would ask that of any other set of symptoms that appear together, but now we are talking about the body politic instead of the personal body. What is the anxiety about the loss of productivity? What is the fear of depression that haunts the society?

Barbara Bush wrote in her memoir that she was "very depressed, lonely, and unhappy" and "hid these feelings from everyone...but George."[118] She felt guilty. She thought that "you could control your emotions and that you just needed to think of others and not just yourself."[119] She wrote in her book that she had no reason to be depressed at fifty-one. What her age has to do with the reason to be depressed I do not quite know, but she said she had no reason to be depressed when she was fifty-one, when her husband was taking over the CIA. "I had a husband whom I adored, the world's greatest children, more friends than I could see...I could not share in George's job after years of being so involved."[120] In other words, she is attributed her depression to the facts that his moving into the CIA kept the two of them more distant and the children were leaving home. As she says, "our children were all gone."[121] I think there could be a psychic relation between being the wife of the director of the CIA and being depressed. I think it is extremely serious to know what your work is and what your spouse's work is and how you are contributing to whatever is

---

117. Morris W. Brody, *Observations on Direct Analysis: The Therapeutic Technique of Dr. John N. Rosen* (New York: Vantage Press, 1959).

118. Barbara Bush, *A Memoir* (New York: A Lisa Drew Book/Scribner, 2010 [1994]), 137.

119. Ibid., 138.

120. Ibid.

121. Ibid.

going on in the world that you hate and bitch about. And I do not think voting and recycling does it. I think there is a lot more to do.

This is a little ad from a New York newspaper—I tell you, this really is my Mort Sahl day—that says: "Depressed? Free treatment is available for participants in a research study with known anti-depressants." Come on in and get your free Prozac. "Depression evaluation service affiliated with Columbia Presbyterian Medical Center both in New York City and Westchester. All calls are confidential." So maybe the recovery movement will move from eating and drinking to depression, and we will discover that all those other troubles are really at root depression. That is the way our society thinks: now we have really got to the bottom of it— it is depression!

In *The Menninger Letter* of October 1994,[122] it says, in the inside column, "Rate of Depression Higher than Thought." There is more depression in the society than we had thought. This is this notion that it is now an epidemic problem. "The highest rate of depression," the findings say, "was in African American women between 35 and 44," "Hispanics were affected twice as frequently as African Americans," and "the lowest prevalence occurred later in life, after 45." Which is very interesting because it used to be thought that depression belonged to older age. Now it is found to be the mostly in the middle-aged realm of African American and Hispanics. What we white people call minorities. So what does it mean if the minorities are depressed, and depression is bad for the country? What are we gonna do? We are going to drug 'em or shock 'em to get them back in the system, and also to keep them, adapted or adjusted or what? Out of sight? Docile?

The researchers identified several significant factors related to major depression: being female—well that takes care of over half the people—less well educated, and separated, widowed, divorced, or never married. You see, we are talking about those who are oppressed by the society—those that are outcasts, left alone, exiled, singled, who do not fit into a certain pattern. Instead of seeing this as a social or political or economic problem, it becomes a psychological problem, and eventually a *brain* problem. About serotonin. So depression becomes wholly individual and interiorized, your

122. A monthly newsletter from the Menninger Clinic, Topeka, Kansas.

personal sickness. Not social or political. "Respondents who reported their employment class as 'homemaker' or 'other' also were at greater risk."

Here's another little booklet—by the way, the materials from the National Institute of Mental Health are printed in yellow. Those of you know something about color symbolism will know that yellow is the brightest color, with the most saturation, and the most visible. So these are, so to speak, cheerful publications. But yellow is the color of lots of other things as well, like decay and cowardliness, so there is a whole other side to yellow, of course. In the descriptions of depression it says: "Over 15 million Americans suffer from depressive illnesses." "Depressive illnesses can take a staggering toll." "They cause great pain to millions of people." Yes. "The lives of family and friends are affected, often seriously disrupted." Yes. "They hurt the economy costing an estimated 30 billion in 1990." Then the trick of it all: "Many do not recognize their illness." We do not know what is happening to us until someone tells us that we are depressed. "Many do not recognize their illness. Nearly two thirds of depressed people do not get appropriate treatment because their symptoms are not recognized...are blamed on personal weakness...are so disabling that people cannot reach out for help." That is, of course, true, that it is disabling. And then that these people "are misdiagnosed and wrongly treated."

I do not want to get into the business of misdiagnosis. That is such an enormously complex question, and there have been so many studies showing that the same person within one week can be diagnosed by two teams of diagnosticians in different hospitals with completely different diagnoses. The question of diagnosis is so obscurely difficult that, of course, people get misdiagnosed. But the word *misdiagnosed* assumes that there is a *true* diagnosis rather than that a diagnosis is a *working hypothesis*. It is a framework you can use for certain procedures that follow from that diagnosis. It is not a statement of truth of what a person is or has in the mental realm, generally speaking. So misdiagnosis assumes there is true and false diagnosis, whereas it should be a question of which working hypothesis you are going to use in a particular case. What is in the foreground? What is in the background? Because that is what a diagnosis does, elevating certain phenomena to the foreground and allowing others to be in the background.

*Anti-Depressants*

There is something about feeling the weight of the world. That if you are not depressed with the fish turning belly up in the rivers and the trees being chopped down left and right and the rest of it, you are not living. How could the soul—your soul—not be sensitive to the soul of the world? That is one of the oldest ideas that we have in Western thought, that the soul of the world and the soul of the human being are interconnected. Our individualism has isolated the soul of the individual, so that we can live completely in a theory that keeps it apart, as if it is in a box. But if someone says that after getting off an anti-depressant he began to feel again, he began to feel the weight of the world, then I would say that his soul has returned.

Prozac is the new fashion, but like any new fashion, it overextends into the whole culture, and then it becomes "the thing," so that we have lots of books about it, and then that, too, will pass. Then we will crystallize what the residues of it are. My focus is not only on Prozac. My focus is mainly on the place of depression in a manic society, and on a manic society that requires a certain kind of political life, the kind we have had so far: unbridled, or what is called "free" enterprise. Unbridled profiteering is another phrase for it, in which the slaves vote for the masters. And with the slaves depotentiated, one way or another, there will not be change, unless there is change from above. Usually, revolutions are from below, and I still regard therapy as a revolutionary activity, a subversive activity that began with Freud. A secret, subversive activity in which the patient's identity was kept hidden and concealed. We still practice that by not using names and disguising our cases. There is something subversive about it. I worry about it, when it becomes an activity of the state. I am trying to point out that we are in a state that lies to us when we are supposed to tell the truth, and we do not deal with it by voting somebody out of office, and we do not deal with it by saying that the whole thing stinks. That is far too childishly easy. Lifton calls it psychic numbing.[123] How do you awaken from numbing? It is as old as Plato: you are in the cave looking at illusions. How do you awaken from the cave? How do you begin to

---

123. Robert Jay Lifton, "Beyond Psychic Numbing: A Call to Awareness," *American Journal of Orthopsychiatry* 52, no. 4 (October 1982).

realize that what you are looking at are illusions? How can one begin to make changes?

Now I have held that, in some way, staying true to depression, and trying to live it, trying to find out what it wants, being interested in it, may be more revolutionary than we realize. It may be more of a political act than we realize. There are things in the depression that could possibly connect you beyond your own misery. That would be a more alchemical view of it too, where the black begins to turn into blue, where it becomes a communicable disease rather than an isolating disease, and where a certain sensitivity can occur from this sickness, this denseness, and this inured leaden nothing. Because we are still left having to ask *beyond the physiological.* What does it want? Because, psychologically, we are obliged to ask that of everything whether it is an appendicitis or a nose bleed, we are obliged, psychologically, to ask, What does it want? and we are not *allowed,* psychologically, to relegate anything to the body *only.* There is no such thing *psychologically* as *only* body or *only* world or *only* matter. That is the meaning of psychic reality. It does not mean that we are making a positive statement that psyche is in all these things, but as a psychologist our attitude is always, What else is going on here for the psyche, for the soul? It is not a metaphysical statement but a psychological attitude.

Now the argument about treatment should not only be a question of pharmacology, because then we are split into the old wars of body versus mind, and I do not want to do that at all. I am thinking of a case that I know where the man lived a very manic life, and when depressions hit him, he found them unbearable, and he had very little ability to deal with them. He was a writer. He was seeing a psychiatrist, and he went on Prozac for a while. He was very grateful for it because as he said it put a floor underneath him, so that when he went down, he did not drop below a certain level. But he kicked it after, I forget, six months or so, because it also put a ceiling on him. He wanted to write, and the ceiling prevented him from writing. The floor was tremendously beneficial, but he did not like the ceiling.

I do not think that we will ever set up depression centers where people can cop out for six months. This is where the problem of case management comes in. How can you help a person enter the world in the most modest way possible for the sake of the depression rather than for the sake of the manic values? In other words, how can you take sides with the depression? What will the depression allow this person to do? What is the absolute minimum? How can this depression find at least just that little bit of space?

To be for or against is sort of absolutism thinking. It is not your job as therapist to condone or repair. You do not have to lighten the depression. Those alternatives are part of depressive thinking. So by recognizing that this is the way the *nigredo* thinks, you do not have to share that thinking pattern, but you can at least in some way show that identification. The difficulty in all therapy is identification of what we call *literalization*—literalizing the condition—and until it is freed a little bit, it is pretty hard to do. But it is not the only thing that gets literalized. The manic condition, all the conditions, everything—the gods tend to possess us intensely, and we literalize what the message is. We fall in love because it is got to be. In that kind of really bleak place, where there is no possibility of moving the thought at all—one of the writers on suicide said it is false thinking—as if you could just change your thoughts—but his point was correct. There is literalization or a psychotic concretization of thought that makes it very difficult to reframe this. And in that case, when it happens like that, it may need medication, which is the only thing outside of that box.

And there is also something about who doses and when and where. We only think of drugs as a piece of white stuff—so many grams and all—people are the same and all have the same effects. We are thinking mechanistically and materialistically. Drugs always have a person involved, and a time and a purpose and a state of soul.

Perhaps I can further clarify my problems with psychopharmacology. It is not that I am opposing psyche to matter or mind to body, or saying that if you are a psychotherapist, you must never use drugs. You know, being the opposite of a materialist is to be a materialist. That is not the point. The point is that you can do psychological work in any kind of condition, within the limits of that condition. There is always the opportunity to think and work psychologically, as psyche is always available to you. You do not have to close out a whole lot of things in order to do psyche. But there is a problem in the *thinking* of psychopharmacology, in its theories that locate the disorder inside the person and inside the brain. Now locating it inside the person returns the problem of depression to the individual and omits or leaves out enough consideration of the societal or of the spirit of the times. It becomes *my* depression again rather than a reflection of the depression of the world or the depression of the landscape or the depression of our sociopolitical history. So it loses its meaning as a reflection of the world soul and becomes only a disorder of my personal serotonin level. And unless the brain physiology is related in some way to the world, it still remains within my skin and is trapped in individualistic theory. This is what I am opposing mainly, the individualism of it.

The function of the therapist is, of course, with the individual and with relieving the individual of the individual's disease. But the function of the thinker, of the theorist, is different. I want to make that clear. I am not engaged now in the treatment of a patient. When I am treating a patient, I will tend to focus on the individual patient, and first of all do no harm and try to remember what was said about Apollo: *He who hastens to help.* That was a motto of Apollo. He is the father of Asclepius, the god of medicine. But we still need to consider the theoretical aspects of what it means to locate a disorder in an individual.

I would say that all depression is biological. Every breath I take is biological, but it is also, at the same time, social or political. It depends on what we are putting in the foreground and what the patient is presenting as the foreground.

Another aspect of the psychopharmacology is that there is a fascination with chemical change. We now call it chemical dependency. But the human being is fascinated by extraordinary substances that are produced in obscure ways and are presented in small dosages. This has been going on for a very long time, whether it is mushrooms or coffee. These magical potions are very fascinating, and we do not understand fully the psychic power of magical potions. In medicine, it is often said, Be sure you take the drug when it first comes out, because in four years it will not be as effective. Supposedly, there is a decline in the effectiveness of the drug, and that is not only because the bacteria changed, because we are not only talking about resistant strains of bacteria now, we are talking about the effectiveness of the magic. We human beings are very susceptible to the magic of the pill. All I am saying is that this is part of what goes on psychologically in our captivation by pharmacological thinking. The magic suits something in us. And the third part is that it reinforces our notion of individualism, that somehow whatever is going on that is disturbing me is *me*. This is where the pharmacological view and the psychological view share the philosophy of individualism that it is *inside you*. Whether it is inside you psychologically, in your history, or inside you and your body, it is inside *you*, and that is where you have to go to deal with it. And I am suggesting that it is not *only* inside you, and that what goes on inside you is part of the world soul. The point is that the world soul and the human soul are intimately reflecting each other and are connected.

And now we have one more question that was brought up before and that is this question of hope and hopelessness. I want to be very clear that to be without hope does not mean that you are not cheerful or optimistic. Optimism is seeing the bright side of what happens. It is not necessarily talking about the future or what could happen or might happen. It is just whatever happens—the soup is too hot and you burn your tongue, but it is good. There is a sense that whatever happens, happens for the best. It is seeing the bright side of it, not seeing necessarily the shadow of it. So first, hope is not the same as optimism. In fact, it is an enormous relief not to be bothered with hope. And secondly, it does not mean not working idealistically, or having ideals, or applying ideals or having ideals behind all the things you do. Not that these ideals are programs or things to be achieved, but without the ideals you are in trouble. Not hope, but *idealism* is the crucial thing. Some vision, some *something* that has a beauty to it. It is your *ideals* that are offended by what goes on. The ideals of what we love, what makes us do and respond. The ideals are crucial. It does not have anything to do with hope though. When you begin to hope that those ideals can be realized, then you are caught in the whole effort of burnout and disappointment, bitterness, and cynicism, and you say, "Ah fuck that, I am not going to have anything more to do with politics! I am not going to vote—look at it, it is all crap." It is when you lose your ideals that you are in trouble.

### *The* via longissima

One of the amazing things about psychoanalysis was that it did not promise a magical cure. It promised a *via longissima*. So it was much more in the tradition of a discipline than it was in the tradition of a cure. And sometimes we lose that. In the beginning of Jung's *Psychology and Alchemy*,[124] in the introduction to it, he lists a dozen different reasons why therapy can come to an end, and the last one is this: that it can. Freud talked about "analysis terminable or interminable."[125] There is a kind of psychological work that some people are called to that can go on a very long time, and is a great and special thing—a special calling. And there are special people who do that kind of work.

It is in the tradition of a discipline—the years that you had to sign up with the Freudians, or Jung's sense of the *via longissima*.[126] I have been in a case seminar where one of the senior analysts presented a case that she had been working with for twenty-seven years. And many of you have probably been in one therapy or another for ten years. That is not so unusual. That is a tradition of education, not a tradition of cure. And that is why I began by talking about clinical education rather than training. And why I am coming back to the same thing again, which has to do with *soul-making*.

Being an elusive, mercurial deconstructionist, I try to avoid ontological questions such as what *soul* is because there is a presumption in ontological questions that you can pin down something and know its true nature. It seems to me that in the language by means of which the soul speaks, if there is a soul, the metaphors and images do not speak ontologically. In *Suicide and the Soul*, I tried to refuse to answer that substantive question which hypothesizes the soul as a thing that can be defined beyond the way we speak of it, the way we feel it, the way it is used in language. It is like soul food. No one asks, What is soul food? and asks for the definition! What is soul music? What are soulful eyes? What is a person who has lost his soul? What is it if the soul is in distress? What is it if you've sold your soul? Those phrases all carry impact without any kind metaphysical definition, and that is how I use the term. I use the term much more in the way of poetic language or a kind of street language, like "soul brother." In a few places I do use a kind of substantive construction

---

124. *CW* 13: 3.

125. "Analysis Terminable and Interminable" (1937), in *The Standard Edition of the Complete Psychologivcal Works of Sigmund Freud*, translated by James Strachey, vol. 23 (London: The Hogarth Press and the Institute of Psycho-Analysis, 1964).

126. *CW* 13: 6.

and say "the soul" that turns events into experiences, has a concern with love, or is expressed in love, has a concern with death, or is tied up with ideas of death, has a religious concern, is in need of or in search of spirit, or is paired with spirit in some strange way. So there are some terms I use in trying to form a territory without definite borders. The idea that soul provides a perspective suggests that it is a psychological term and a psychological idea by means of which we look at our lives. You can look at your life soullessly without ever considering the word soul and you end up with much of the way we live. If you begin to consider soul as a perspective, then it means looking at what happens, the events of your life, in terms of this imprecise, yet eternally important idea, soul.

Soul-making is not concerned with a cure. That could make a difference in the psychiatric job where you have a patient who is suffering—the Apollonic fantasy of hastening to help—you have got to do something. First of all, do no harm. And that produces all these constant conflicts between medicine, therapy, and soul. It is not that they are essentially at conflict, because they are all in the same human being and in the same world, but these philosophical traditions are very different, and it is important to know what tree you are on and what your work is. Managed care and the insurance companies are forcing therapy into the acute medical model of doing something within the short term. And this is again how the economy is killing the entire world—because everything is done for economic reasons. And this throws into question the discipline that we come from—from Freud and Jung, the long term, the alchemical *via longissima,* the longest way, not the shortcut, how does that fit in? Who is going to pay for it? Maybe only if it turned into education. Teaching or discipline and schooling rather than the realm of curing in the modern sense of healing. I have never used the word healing because I have never been healed, and I do not know what healing is. But I do understand something about sophistication, about education, about subtilization, if you will. I see that as soul-making, but I do not see that necessarily as healing.

What you need to understand is the way I work. I am never concerned about the first shoe. The first shoe is the comfortable shoe. We all know that. We all know that we have freedom of speech, to a certain extent. We all know that we have media access, thirty-five channels or more. We all know what works in this country or in this society. I am interested in the second shoe. It is the same way with therapy. We all know that therapy does this and that and is good. We all know that AA has recovered thousands of people from a horrible life, if not from death. That is no longer interesting. What is interesting is what we do not know, the second shoe. The uncomfortable shoe. The shoe that pinches. I do not want to talk about what we all know. What is the use of talking about the goodness of therapy? Everybody knows how good it is. All the therapists can tell you that! They all can tell you cases that have improved extraordinarily. I am interested in the shadow, the unconscious part. My job is a therapy of ideas. And in order to do a therapy of ideas, you have to lift repression, you have to attack, you have to use acid, you have to use all those alchemical materials that are burning, caustic, and destructive. Because that is the angle that I come at things from. It is an extremist angle. My interest is to make people uncomfortable. To make that first shoe more and more aware of that second shoe. So my hope would be, if I am allowed to use that word, that you have become more uncomfortable, and that I have become more uncomfortable too.

I have been asking the question, Does the soul want something with depression or by means of depression? Is there a purpose at work? Is it an attempt to move from depression, a clinical secular word, to melancholy, a word that involves beauty, the gods, mythology, philosophy, vision, and the *furor melancholicus*? Does the depression *really* want melancholy? In other words, something is there that is of great value, but as long as it is seen only secularly, mechanically, biologically, it does not achieve its aim. The aim is the restoration of melancholy to the society, and that would mean a change in the society, a change in the values of the society. I do not think we can say it any clearer than that. So that sort of sums up what we have been doing and allows us to go home.